Sumerian Myth...

MAN'S GOLDEN AGE

This tablet (29.16.422 in the Nippur collection of the University Museum) is one of the unpublished pieces belonging to the Sumerian epic poem [1] whose hero Enmerkar ruled in the city of Erech sometime during the fourth millennium B. C. The passage enclosed by the black line describes the blissful and unrivalled state of man in an era of universal peace before he had learned to know fear and before the "confusion of tongues"; its contents,[2] which are very reminiscent of Genesis XI:1, read as follows:

In those days there was no snake, there was no scorpion, there was no *hyena*,
There was no lion, there was no *wild dog*, no wolf,
There was no fear, no terror,
Man had no rival.

In those days the land Shubur (East), the place of plenty, of righteous decrees,
Harmony-tongued Sumer (South), the great land of the "decrees of princeship,"
Uri (North), the land having all that is *needful*,
The land Martu (West), resting in security,
The whole universe, the people *in unison*,
To Enlil in one tongue *gave praise*.

SUMERIAN MYTHOLOGY

A Study of Spiritual and Literary Achievement in the Third Millennium B.C.

SAMUEL NOAH KRAMER

REVISED EDITION

HARPER & ROW, PUBLISHERS
New York, Evanston, and London

To My Wife

This book was first published in 1944 by The American Philosophical Society, Philadelphia, and is here reprinted, with revisions, by arrangement.

Research for this essay was supported by grants from the Eldridge Reeves Johnson Fund of The American Philosophical Society. Original publication was aided by a grant from the Jayne Memorial Foundation.

First HARPER PAPERBACK edition published 1961

PREFACE

The Sumerians were a non-Semitic, non-Indo-European people who flourished in southern Babylonia from the beginning of the fourth to the end of the third millenium B. C. During this long stretch of time the Sumerians, whose racial and linguistic affiliations are still unclassifiable, represented the dominant cultural group of the entire Near East. This cultural dominance manifested itself in three directions:

1. It was the Sumerians who developed and probably invented the cuneiform system of writing which was adopted by nearly all the peoples of the Near East and without which the cultural progress of western Asia would have been largely impossible.

2. The Sumerians developed religious and spiritual concepts together with a remarkably well integrated pantheon which influenced profoundly all the peoples of the Near East, including the Hebrews and the Greeks. Moreover, by way of Judaism, Christianity, and Mohammedanism, not a few of these spiritual and religious concepts have permeated the modern civilized world.

3. The Sumerians produced a vast and highly developed literature, largely poetic in character, consisting of epics and myths, hymns and lamentations, proverbs and "words of wisdom." These compositions are inscribed in cuneiform script on clay tablets which date largely from approximately 1750 B. C.[a] In the course of the past hundred years approximately five[b] thousand such literary pieces have been excavated in the mounds of ancient Sumer. Of this number, *over two thousand*, more than two-thirds of our source material, were excavated by the University of Pennsylvania in the mound covering ancient Nippur in the course of four grueling campaigns lasting from 1889 to 1900; these Nippur tablets and fragments represent, therefore, the ma-

jor source for the reconstruction of the Sumerian compositions. As literary products, these Sumerian compositions
rank high among the creations of civilized man. They compare not unfavorably with the ancient Greek and Hebrew
masterpieces, and like them mirror the spiritual and intellectual life of an otherwise little known civilization. Their
significance for a proper appraisal of the cultural and
spiritual development of the Near East can hardly be
overestimated. The Assyrians and Babylonians took them
over almost in toto. The Hittites translated them into
their own language and no doubt imitated them widely.
The form and contents of the Hebrew literary creations and
to a certain extent even those of the ancient Greeks were
profoundly influenced by them. As practically *the oldest
written literature of any significant amount ever uncovered,*
it furnishes new, rich, and unexpected source material to
the archaeologist and anthropologist, to the ethnologist and
student of folklore, to the students of the history of religion
and of the history of literature.

In spite of their unique and extraordinary significance,
and although the large majority of the tablets on which they
were inscribed were excavated almost half a century ago,
the translation and interpretation of the Sumerian literary
compositions have made relatively little progress to date.
The translation of Sumerian is a highly complicated process. It is only in comparatively recent years that the grammar has been scientifically established, while the lexical problems are still numerous and far from resolved. By far the
major obstacle to a trustworthy reconstruction and translation of the compositions, however, is the fact that the
greater part of the tablets and fragments on which they are
inscribed, and which are now largely located in the Museum
of the Ancient Orient at Istanbul and in the University Museum at Philadelphia, have been lying about uncopied and
unpublished, and thus unavailable for study. To remedy
this situation, I travelled to Istanbul in 1937, and, with the
aid of a Guggenheim fellowship, devoted some twenty
months to the copying of 170 tablets and fragments in the

Nippur collection of the Museum of the Ancient Orient. And largely with the help of a grant from the American Philosophical Society, the better part of the past three years has been devoted to the studying of the unpublished literary pieces in the Nippur collection of the University Museum; their copying has already begun.[c]

It is the utilization of this vast quantity of unpublished Sumerian literary tablets and fragments in the University Museum, approximately 675 pieces according to my investigations, which will make possible the restoration and translation of the Sumerian literary compositions and lay the groundwork for a study of Sumerian culture, especially in its more spiritual aspects; a study which, considering the age of the culture involved, that of the third millennium B. C., will long remain unparalleled for breadth of scope and fullness of detail. As the writer visualizes it, the preparation and publication of this survey would be most effective in the form of a seven-volume series bearing the general title, *Studies in Sumerian Culture.* The first volume, the present *Memoir,* is therefore largely introductory in character; it contains a detailed description of our sources together with a brief outline of the more significant mythological concepts of the Sumerians as evident from their epics and myths.

The five subsequent volumes, as planned by the author, will consist primarily of source material, that is, they will contain the transliterated texts of the restored Sumerian compositions, together with a translation and commentary as well as the autograph copies of all the pertinent uncopied material in the University Museum utilized for the reconstruction of the texts. Each of these five volumes will be devoted to a particular class of Sumerian composition: (1) epics; (2) myths; (3) hymns; (4) lamentations; (5) "wisdom." It cannot be too strongly stressed that on the day this task is completed and Sumerian literature is restored and made available to scholar and layman, the humanities will be enriched by one of the most magnificent groups of documents ever brought to light. As the earliest

creative writings, these documents hold a unique position
in the history of civilization. Moreover, because of their
profound and enduring influence on the spiritual and religious development of the entire Near East, they are
veritable untapped mines and treasure-houses of significant source material and invaluable data ready for exploi-
tation by all the relevant humanities.

The seventh volume, *Sumerian Religion: A Comparative
Study,* intended as the last of the series, will sketch the
religious and spiritual concepts of the Sumerians as revealed in their own literature. Moreover, it will endeavor
to trace the influence of these Sumerian concepts on the
spiritual and cultural development of the entire Near East.
This work is left to the last for cogent if obvious reasons;
it is only after the Sumerian literary compositions have
been scientifically reconstructed and trustworthily translated that we shall be in a position to treat adequately and
with reasonable certainty that all-important but very difficult and complicated subject. While, then, the first six
volumes are to contain primarily the data and the sources,
it is the seventh which will attempt to formulate the results
and the conclusions for the historian and the layman. And
the hope is not unjustified that, as a result of this method
of preparation and publication, the final formulation will
prove both significant and reliable.

I wish to express my sincerest and most heartfelt
thanks to the Jayne Memorial Foundation and its board
of trustees, which selected me as the annual lecturer for
1942 to speak on the subject of Sumerian mythology. I
also acknowledge my gratitude to the board of managers
of the University Museum; to Dr. George C. Vaillant, its
director; to Mr. Horace H. F. Jayne, his predecessor; and
to Professor Leon Legrain, the curator of its Babylonian
section, for their scientific co-operation in making the Sumerian literary tablets available to me for study. Profound thanks are due to the Ministry of Education of the
Turkish Republic and its Department of Antiquities, for
permitting me to study and copy part of the Sumerian

literary tablets in the Nippur collection of the Museum of the Ancient Orient at Istanbul. The Oriental Seminar of the University of Pennsylvania acted in a sense as a sounding board for the reading of the first draft of the contents of this study; the spontaneous interest and enthusiasm with which it was received by the participating students and colleagues were of considerable spiritual support in the intricate and at times almost despairing process of penetrating the meaning of the texts. In the matter of financial support I am deeply indebted to the John Simon Guggenheim Memorial Foundation for selecting me as one of its fellows for the years 1937–38 and 1938–39; it thus enabled me to travel to Istanbul and devote some twenty months to research activity in its Museum of the Ancient Orient. To the Oriental Institute of the University of Chicago I am indebted for several minor financial contributions. But primarily it is the American Philosophical Society which has made the preparation of this study possible; it is the extraordinary vision and generosity of this society which is enabling me to reconstruct and translate in a scientific and trustworthy manner the extant Sumerian literary compositions; to piece together and recover for the world at large the oldest literature ever uncovered, and one of the most significant.

To the Macmillan Company and the University of Chicago Press I am indebted for permission to reproduce several illustrations; specific acknowledgment of this courtesy is made in the captions of plates V, VII, X, XII, XIV, and XIX.

NOTE

References and Notes to the original edition will be found on page 104. Supplementary Notes and Corrections will be found on page 120.

CONTENTS

LIST OF ILLUSTRATIONS

PLATES

TEXT FIGURES

MAP

xiv

Sumerian Mythology

INTRODUCTION

THE SOURCES: THE SUMERIAN LITERARY TABLETS DATING FROM APPROXIMATELY 2000 B. C.

The study of Sumerian culture introduced by the present volume, *Sumerian Mythology,* is to be based largely on Sumerian literary sources; it will consist of the formulation of the spiritual and religious concepts of the Sumerians, together with the reconstructed text and translation of the Sumerian literary compositions in which these concepts are revealed. It is therefore very essential that the reader have a clear picture of the nature of our source material, which consists primarily of some three thousand tablets and fragments inscribed in the Sumerian language and dated approximately 1750 B. C.[a] It is the first aim of the Introduction of the present volume to achieve such clarification. It therefore begins with a brief sketch of the rather rocky road leading to the decipherment of the Sumerian language and continues with a brief résumé of the excavations conducted on various Sumerian sites in the course of the past three-quarters of a century. After a very brief general evaluation of the contents of the huge mass of Sumerian tablet material uncovered in the course of these excavations, it turns to the Sumerian literary tablets which represent the basic material for our study, and analyzes in some detail the scope and date of their contents. The Introduction then concludes with a description of the factors which prevented in large part the trustworthy reconstruction and translation of the Sumerian literary compositions in the past; the details, not uninteresting in themselves, furnish a revealing and illuminating commentary on the course and progress of one of the more significant humanistic efforts of our generation.

The decipherment of Sumerian differed from that of Accadian[s] and Egyptian in one significant detail, a detail which proved to be one of the factors in hampering the progress of Sumerology to no inconsiderable extent. For in the case of Egypt, Assyria, and Babylonia, the investigating scholars of western Europe had at their disposal much relevant material from Biblical, classical, and post-classical sources. Not only were such names as Egypt, Ashur, and Babylon well known, but at least to a certain extent and with much limitation and qualification, even the culture of the peoples was not altogether unfamiliar. In the case of the Sumerians, however, the situation was quite different; *there was no clearly recognizable trace of Sumer or its people and language in the entire Biblical, classical, and post-classical literature.* The very name Sumer was erased from the mind and memory of man for over two thousand years. The discovery of the Sumerians and their language came quite unexpectedly and was quite unlooked for; and this more or less irrelevant detail was at least partially responsible for the troubled progress of Sumerology from the earliest days to the present moment.

Historically, the decipherment of Sumerian resulted from that of Accadian, which in turn followed the decipherment of cuneiform Persian. Briefly sketched, the process was as follows. In 1765, the Danish traveler and scholar, Carsten Niebuhr, succeeded in making careful copies of several inscriptions on the monuments of Persepolis. These were published between the years 1774 and 1778, and were soon recognized as trilingual, that is, the same inscriptions seemed to be repeated in three different languages. It was not unreasonable to assume, since the monuments were located in Persepolis, that they were inscribed by one or more kings of the Achaemenid dynasty and that the first version in each inscription was in the Persian language. Fortunately, at approximately the same time, Old Persian was becoming known to western European scholars through the efforts of Duperron, who had studied in India under the Parsees and was preparing translations of the Avesta. And so by 1802, with the help of the newly acquired knowledge of Old Persian and by keen manipulation of the

Achaemenid proper names as handed down in Biblical and classical literature, the German scholar, Grotefend, succeeded in deciphering a large part of the Persian version of the inscriptions. Additions and corrections were made by numerous scholars in the ensuing years. But the crowning achievement belongs to the Englishman H. C. Rawlinson. A member of the English Intelligence Service, Rawlinson was first stationed in India, where he mastered the Persian language. In 1835 he was transferred to Persia, where he learned of the huge trilingual inscription on the rock of Behistun and determined to copy it. The Persian version of the Behistun inscription consists of 414 lines; the second, now known as the Elamite version, consists of 263 lines; while the third, the Accadian (designated in earlier Assyriological literature as Assyrian or Babylonian—see note 3) version, consists of 112 lines. During the years 1835–37, at the risk of life and limb, Rawlinson succeeded in copying 200 lines of the Persian version. He returned in 1844 and completed the copying of the Persian as well as the Elamite version. The Accadian inscription, however, was so situated that it was impossible for him to copy it, and it was not until 1847 that he succeeded in making squeezes of the text. To return to the decipherment of cuneiform Persian, by 1846 Rawlinson published his memoir in the *Journal of the Royal Asiatic Society,* which gave the transliteration and translation of the Persian version of the Behistun inscription together with a copy of the cuneiform original.

Long before the final decipherment of the Persian text, however, great interest had been aroused in western Europe by the third version of the Persepolis inscriptions. For it was soon recognized that this was the script and language found in numerous inscriptions and bricks, clay tablets, and clay cylinders which were finding their way into Europe from sites that might well be identified with Nineveh and Babylon. In 1842 the French under Botta began the excavation of Khorsabad, and in 1845 Layard began his excavations of Nimrud and Nineveh. Inscribed monuments were being found in large quantities at all three sites; moreover,

Layard was uncovering at Nineveh a large number of inscribed clay tablets. By 1850, therefore, Europe had scores of inscriptions coming largely from Assyrian sites, made in the very same script and language as the third version of the Persepolis and Behistun inscriptions. The decipherment of this language was simplified on the one hand by the fact that it was recognized quite early in the process that it belonged to the Semitic group of languages. On the other hand, it was complicated by the fact that the orthography, as was soon recognized, was syllabic and ideographic rather than alphabetic. The leading figure in the decipherment of Accadian, or Assyrian as it was then designated, was the Irish scholar Edward Hincks. But once again a major contribution was made by Rawlinson. In 1851 he published the text, transliteration, and translation of the Accadian version of the Behistun inscription, the large trilingual to whose text he alone had access.

As for the second, or Elamite version, of the Behistun inscription, it offered relatively little difficulty as soon as progress was made in the decipherment of Accadian, since it uses a syllabary based on the Accadian system of writing. The major figures in its decipherment were Westergaard and Norris. As early as 1855 Norris, the secretary of the Royal Asiatic Society, published the complete text of the second version of the Behistun inscription, which had been copied by Rawlinson, together with a transliteration and a translation; this remained practically the standard work on the subject until Weissbach published his *Achämenideninschriften zweiter Art* in 1896.

As will be noted, nothing has yet been heard or said of the Sumerians. As early as 1850, however, Hincks began to doubt that the Semitic inhabitants of Assyria and Babylonia had invented the cuneiform system of writing. In the Semitic languages the stable element is the consonant while the vowel is extremely variable. It seemed unnatural, therefore, that the Semites should invent a syllabic system of orthography in which the vowel seemed to be as unchanging as the consonant. Moreover, if the Semites had invented the script, one might have expected to be able to trace the syllabic values of the signs to Semitic words. But this was hardly ever the case; the syllabic values all seemed to go back to words or elements for which no Semitic equivalent could be found. Hincks thus began to suspect that the cuneiform system of writing was invented by a non-Semitic people who had preceded the Semites in Mesopotamia. In 1855 Rawlinson published a memoir in the *Journal of the Royal Asiatic Society* in which he speaks of his discovery of non-Semitic inscriptions on bricks and tablets from sites in southern Babylonia such as Nippur, Larsa, and Erech. In 1856 Hincks took up the problem of this new language, recognized that it was agglutinative in character, and gave the first examples from bilinguals which had come to the British Museum from the Nineveh excavations. The name of the language was variously designated as Scythic or even Accadian, that is, the very name now given to the Semitic tongue spoken in Assyria and Babylonia. In 1869, however, the French scholar Oppert, basing himself on the royal title, "king of Sumer and Accad," and realizing that Accad referred to the land inhabited by the Semitic population, rightly attributed the name Sumerian to the language spoken by the non-Semitic people who had invented the cuneiform script. Nevertheless, Oppert was not immediately followed by the majority of the Assyriologists, and the name Accadian continued to be used for Sumerian for many years.[5]

For several decades following the discovery of the existence of Sumerian, practically all the source material for its decipherment and study consisted of the bilinguals and syllabaries from the so-called Ashurbanipal library which was discovered and excavated at Nineveh. This material dates from the seventh century B. C., some fifteen hundred years after the disappearance of Sumer as a political entity. As for the material from the Sumerian sites, it consisted almost entirely of a very small group of bricks, tablets, and cylinders from the Sumerian and post-Sumerian periods which had found their way into the British Museum. In

1877, however, began the first successful excavation at a Sumerian site. In that year, the French under De Sarzec began to excavate at Telloh the ancient Sumerian city of

---

MAP 1. SUMER IN THE FIRST HALF OF THE THIRD MILLENNIUM B. C.

The Sumerians were a non-Semitic, non-Indo-European people who probably entered Mesopotamia from the east prior to or during the fourth millennium B. C. At the time of the Sumerian invasion much of the land between the Tigris and the Euphrates Rivers was no doubt inhabited by the Semites, and the entrance of the Sumerians marked the beginning of a struggle between the two peoples for control of the two-river land, which lasted for some two millennia. To judge from our present data, victory first fell to the Sumerians. There is reason to assume that at one time the Sumerians were in control of the better part of Mesopotamia and that they even carried their conquests into more distant lands. It was no doubt during this period of conquest and power in the fourth millennium B. C. that the Sumerians made important advances in their economic, social, and political organization. This material progress, together with the growth and development of the spiritual and religious concepts which accompanied it, must have left an enduring impress on all the peoples of the Near East who came in contact with the Sumerians during the fourth millennium.

But the early defeat of the Semites by the Sumerians did not mark the end of the struggle between the two peoples for the control of Mesopotamia. No doubt with the help of new invasion hordes from the Arabian peninsula, the Semites gradually regained some of their strength and became ever more aggressive. And so in the first part of the third millennium we find the Sumerians being gradually pushed back to the more southerly portion of Mesopotamia, roughly from Nippur to the Persian Gulf on our map. North of Nippur the Semites seemed well entrenched.

Approximately in the middle of the third millennium arose the great Semitic conqueror, Sargon, the founder of the dynasty of Accad. He and the kings that followed him attacked and badly defeated the Sumerians to the south, making it a practice, moreover, to carry off many of their victims into captivity and to settle Semites in their places. This defeat marked the beginning of the end for the Sumerians. It is true that toward the very end of the third millennium the Sumerians made a final attempt at political control of Mesopotamia, and under the so-called "Third Dynasty of Ur" met with a certain initial success. However, the important role played by the Semites even in this "Neo-Sumerian" kingdom, which lasted for no more than a century, is indicated by the fact that the last three kings of the dynasty bore Semitic names. With the destruction of Ur, their last capital, in approximately 2050 B. C., the Sumerians gradually disappeared as a political entity. Not long afterwards, the Amurru, a Semitic people who had begun to penetrate into lower Mesopotamia toward the end of the third millennium, established the city of Babylon as their capital, and under such rulers as Hammurabi succeeded in obtaining temporary sway over Mesopotamia. Because of the prominence of Babylon in the second and first millennia B. C., the country once held and ruled by the Sumerians came to be known as Babylonia, a name which has continued in use to the present day.[4]

(Map drawn by Marie Strobel, after one facing page 643 in *Handbuch der Archäologie* (München, 1939).)

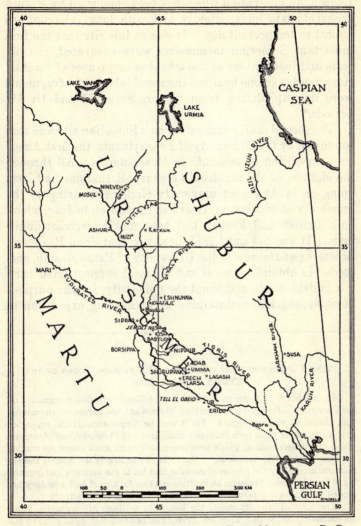

Map 1. Sumer in the First Half of the Third Millennium B. C.

(For description, see opposite page.)

○ Ancient sites, ancient names (in vertical lettering)

○ Ancient sites, modern names (in oblique lettering)

□ Modern sites

Lagash, an excavation which has been conducted by French archaeologists intermittently and with long interruptions almost to the present day. It was at this site that the first important Sumerian monuments were excavated, the objects and inscriptions of the *ishakkus* or princes of Lagash. Here more than one hundred thousand tablets and fragments were dug up, dating from the pre-Sargonid and Ur III periods.[6]

The second major excavation on a Sumerian site was that conducted by the University of Pennsylvania, the first American expedition to excavate in Mesopotamia. All through the eighties of the nineteenth century discussions had been going on in American university circles pertaining to the feasibility of sending an American expedition to Iraq, where both British and French had been making extraordinary finds. It was not until 1887, however, that John P. Peters, professor of Hebrew in the University of Pennsylvania, succeeded in obtaining moral and financial support from various individuals in and about the university, for the purpose of equipping and maintaining an excavating expedition in

---

PLATE I. A SCENE FROM THE NIPPUR EXCAVATIONS: ROOMS OF THE TEMPLE "TABLET HOUSE."

In the history of American archaeology, the Nippur expedition, organized by the University of Pennsylvania more than 50 years ago, will always be remembered with special interest and regard. For it was the Nippur excavations, supported over a number of years by a relatively small group of Philadelphians of unusual vision and understanding, which were responsible to no small extent for making America "archaeology-conscious." Moreover, it was largely the interest and enthusiasm aroused by the Nippur discoveries that led to the founding and organizing of the University Museum, an institution which for almost half a century has proved to be a leading pioneer in all branches of archaeological activity.

The ruins of Nippur, among the largest in southern Mesopotamia, cover approximately 180 acres. They are divided into two well-nigh equal parts by the now dry bed of the Shatt-en-Nil, a canal which at one time branched off from the Euphrates and watered and fructified the otherwise barren territory through which it flowed. The eastern half contains the temple structures, including the ziggurat and the group of buildings which must have formed the scribal school and library; it is in this part of the mound that the "tablet house" was excavated. The western half seems to mark the remains of the city proper.[7]

PLATE I

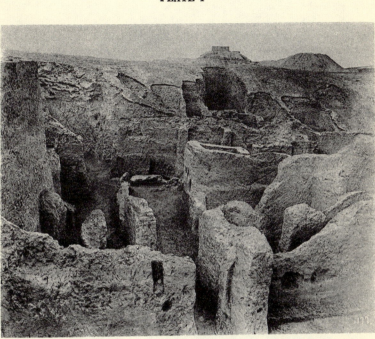

A Scene from the Nippur Excavations: Rooms of the Templf "Tablet House."

(For description, see opposite page.)

Iraq under the auspices of the University of Pennsylvania. Nippur, one of the largest and most important mounds in Iraq, was chosen, and four long and extremely difficult excavating campaigns were conducted during the years 1889–90, 1890–91, 1893–96, and 1896–1900.

The hardships and handicaps were severe and discouraging. One young archaeologist died in the field, and there was hardly a year in which one or the other of the members of the expedition did not suffer from serious illness. Difficulties with the Arab tribes were not infrequent and at times assumed a most threatening character. In spite of the obstacles, however, the excavating continued, and in the course of the four campaigns which lasted more than a decade, the expedition achieved magnificent and in some respects unparalleled results, at least in the inscriptional field. The Nippur expedition succeeded in excavating approximately thirty thousand tablets and fragments in the course of its four campaigns, the larger part of which are inscribed in the Sumerian language and date from the second half of the third millennium to the first half of the second millennium B. C.

The contents of these tablets are rich and varied. The greater part is economic in character; it consists of contracts and bills of sale, promissory notes and receipts, lists and accounts, wills, adoptions, court decisions, and other legal and administrative documents. Many of the tablets are letters; some are historical inscriptions; still others are lexical in character, that is, they contain Sumerian dictionary and grammatical material of priceless value for our study of the language, since they were actually compiled by the ancient scribes themselves. But especially noteworthy is the large group of tablets dated about 1750 B. C.[a] which are inscribed with the Sumerian literary compositions consisting of epics and myths, hymns and laments, proverbs and "wisdom."

After Nippur, the excavations by the Germans at Fara (the ancient "flood" city Shuruppak) in 1902–03 and those by the University of Chicago at Bismaya (ancient

Adab) in 1903–04 uncovered important Sumerian economic and lexical material dating largely from the pre-Sargonid and Sargonid periods in the third millennium B. C. Excavations at Kish, begun by the French in 1911 and continued under Anglo-American auspices from 1922 to 1930, have yielded important inscriptional material. In Jemdet Nasr, not far from Kish, a large group of semi-pictographic tablets that go back to the early beginnings of Sumerian writing were uncovered. Ur, the famous site excavated by a joint expedition of the British Museum and the University Museum between the years 1919 and 1933, yielded many historical and economic inscriptions and some literary material. In Asmar (ancient Eshnunna) and Khafaje, east of the Tigris, a large number of economic tablets dating largely from the Sargonid and Ur III periods, that is, the latter part of the third millennium B. C., were excavated by the Oriental Institute of the University of Chicago in recent years. Finally in Erech, where the Germans conducted excavations from 1928 until the outbreak of the war, a large group of pictographic tablets antedating even those found at Jemdet Nasr has been uncovered.[8]

This brief survey furnishes a bird's-eye view of the Sumerian inscriptional finds uncovered and brought to light by legitimate excavations.[d] In addition, scores of thousands of tablets have been dug up clandestinely by the native Arabs in the mounds of Sumer, especially in the ancient sites of Larsa, Sippar, and Umma. It is therefore difficult to estimate the number of Sumerian tablets and fragments now in the possession of the museums and private collections; *a quarter of a million* is probably a conservative guess. What now is the nature of the contents of this vast accumulation of Sumerian inscriptional material? What significant information can it be expected to reveal?

In the first place it is important to note that *more than ninety-five per cent of all the Sumerian tablets are economic in character*, that is, they consist of notes and receipts, contracts of sale and exchange, agreements of adoption and partnership, wills and testaments, lists of workers and wages, letters, etc. Because these documents follow a more or less expected and traditional pattern which is found also in the Accadian documents of the same character, their translation, except in the more complicated cases, is not too difficult. It is the contents of these tablets which furnish us with a relatively full and accurate picture of the social and economic structure of Sumerian life in the third millennium B. C. Moreover, the large quantity of onomastic material to be found in these economic documents represents a fruitful source for the study of the ethnic distribution in and about Sumer during this period.[9]

Of the Sumerian inscriptions that are not economic in character, one group consists of approximately six hundred building and dedicatory inscriptions on steles, bricks, cones, vases, etc. It is from this relatively small group of inscriptions that the political history of Sumer has been largely recovered. The translation of these inscriptions, too, offers no very great difficulties, since the contents are usually brief and simple. Moreover, the structure and pattern of the Sumerian dedicatory inscriptions are followed to a large extent by the later Accadian building inscriptions; the bilingual material, too, is of considerable help. All in all, therefore, except in the more complex instances, the Sumerian historical material is relatively simple to translate and interpret.[10]

In addition to the economic and historical material described above, there is also a varied and important group of tablets inscribed with lexical and mathematical texts and with incantations.[11] But by far the most significant material for the study of Sumerian culture, especially in its more spiritual aspects, consists of a group of "literary" tablets dated about 1750 B. C. which are inscribed with Sumerian epics and myths, hymns and lamentations, proverbs and "words of wisdom." And it is important to note that, in spite of the vast quantity of Sumerian inscriptional material excavated to date, only some *three thousand* tablets[b] and fragments, no more than one percent, are inscribed with Sumerian literary compositions. Of these three thousand pieces, approximately nine hundred are distributed as follows. Some three hundred very small fragments have been found in Kish by the French and were published by De Genouillac in 1924. Approximately two hundred tablets and fragments were bought by the Berlin Museum from dealers; these were published by Zimmern in 1912-13. Approximately one hundred were acquired by the Louvre from dealers; these were published by De Genouillac in 1930. Less than a hundred pieces have found their way to the British Museum and the Ashmolean Museum; these have been published in the course of several decades by King, Langdon, and Gadd. To these must be added an uncertain number (two hundred?) excavated in Ur which are to be published by Gadd of the British Museum in the near future.[12]

The remaining two thousand and one hundred tablets and fragments, by far the major part of our Sumerian literary tablets, were excavated by the University of Pennsylvania at Nippur some fifty years ago. Of this number, over one hundred have found their way to the University of Jena in Germany; approximately eight hundred are in the possession of the Museum of the Ancient Orient in Istanbul; almost *eleven hundred* are located in the University Museum at Philadelphia. It is no exaggeration to state, therefore, that it is the Nippur expedition of the University of Pennsylvania which is to be credited in large part with the recovery and restoration of the ancient Sumerian literary compositions as written down at approximately 1750 B. C. It is well worth noting that these Sumerian literary creations are significant not only for their remarkable form and illuminating contents. They are unique, too, in that they have come down to us as actually written by the scribes of four thousand years ago, unmodified and uncodified by later redactors with axes to grind and ideologies to satisfy. *Our Sumerian literary compositions thus represent the oldest literature of any appreciable and significant amount ever uncovered.*

Let us now examine very briefly the nature of the contents of this Sumerian literature. As already mentioned, it consists of epics and myths, hymns and lamentations, proverbs and "wisdom" compositions. Of the epic tales at least nine can now be restored in large part. Six of these commemmorate the feats and exploits of the great Sumerian heroes Enmerkar, Lugalbanda, and especially Gilgamesh, the forerunner of the Greek hero Heracles; these three Sumerian heroes lived in all probability toward the end of the fourth and the beginning of the third millennium B. C., fully five thousand years ago. The remaining three epic tales deal with the destruction of Kur, the monstrous creature which at least in a certain sense corresponds to the Babylonian goddess Tiamat, the Hebrew Leviathan, and perhaps the Greek Typhon. As for the myths, their contents, which obviously enough represent the prime source material for our Sumerian mythology, will be sketched with considerable detail in the following chapters. Only the Tammuz myths dealing with the dying deity and his resurrection will be omitted; the contents are still too obscure for reasonably safe interpretation.[13]

The hymns are both royal and divine.[c] The latter consist of songs of praise and exaltation directed to all the more important deities of the Sumerian pantheon; they are quite diversified in size, structure, and content. The royal hymns, frequently self-laudatory in character, were composed largely for the kings of the Third Dynasty of Ur and of the Isin Dynasty which followed it. This is a significant historical fact, for it helps us date the actual composition of much of our Sumerian literature. The Third Dynasty of Ur reigned during the last two centuries of the third millennium B. C.; with the defeat and capture of their last king Ibi-Sin in approximately 2050 B. C. Sumer ceased to exist as a political entity. The kings of the Isin Dynasty which followed were Semites; nevertheless their hymns, like those of their predecessors, were composed and written in Sumerian, which continued to be used as the literary and religious language of the conquerors.[14]

The lamentation is a type of tragic composition developed by the Sumerians to commemorate the frequent destruction of their cities by the surrounding more barbaric peoples; it is the forerunner of such Biblical compositions as the *Book of Lamentations*. One large poem, consisting of more than four hundred lines which lament the destruction of the city of Ur, has already been restored and published,[15] and a similar composition dealing with the destruction of Nippur and its restoration is in the process of being restored. In addition it is now possible to reconstruct large

---

PLATE II. OLDEST LITERARY CATALOGUE

This plate illustrates a literary catalogue compiled in approximately 2000 B. C. (clay tablet 29.15.155 in the Nippur collection of the University Museum). The upper part represents the tablet itself; the lower part, the author's hand copy of the tablet. The titles of those compositions whose actual contents we can now reconstruct in large part are as follows:

1. Hymn of King Shulgi (approximately 2100 B. C.).
2. Hymn of King Lipit-Ishtar (approximately 1950 B. C.).
3. Myth, "The Creation of the Pickax" (see p. 51).
4. Hymn to Inanna, queen of heaven.
5. Hymn to Enlil, the air-god.
6. Hymn to the temple of the mother-goddess Ninhursag in the city of Kesh.
7. Epic tale, "Gilgamesh, Enkidu, and the Nether World" (see p. 30).
8. Epic tale, "Inanna and Ebih" (see p. 82).
9. Epic tale, "Gilgamesh and Huwawa."
10. Epic tale, "Gilgamesh and Agga."
11. Myth, "Cattle and Grain" (see p. 53).
12. Lamentation over the fall of Agade in the time of Naram-Sin (approximately 2400 B. C.).
13. Lamentation over the destruction of Ur. This composition, consisting of 436 lines, has been almost completely reconstructed and published by the author as *Assyriological Study No. 12* of the Oriental Institute of the University of Chicago.
14. Lamentation over the destruction of Nippur.
15. Lamentation over the destruction of Sumer.
16. Epic tale, "Lugalbanda and Enmerkar."
17. Myth, "Inanna's Descent to the Nether World" (see p. 83).
18. Perhaps a hymn to Inanna.
19. Collection of short hymns to all the important temples of Sumer.
20. Wisdom compositions describing the activities of a boy training to be a scribe.
21. Wisdom composition, "Instructions of a Peasant to His Son." [16]

PLATE II

OLDEST LITERARY CATALOGUE

(For description, see opposite page.)

parts of a lamentation over the destruction of Sumer as a whole, and of another that at present may be best described as the "weeping mother" type. Finally we now have the larger part of a composition which laments a calamity that befell the city of Agade during the reign of Naram-Sin who ruled in the earlier part of the second half of the third millennium B. C.[14]

And so we come finally to the wisdom compositions of the Sumerians, the prototypes of the wisdom literature current all over the Near East and exemplified by the Biblical *Book of Proverbs*.[f] Sumerian wisdom literature consists of a large number of brief, pithy, and pointed proverbs and aphorisms; of various fables, such as "The Bird and the Fish," "The Tree and the Reed," "The Pickax and the Plow," "Silver and Bronze"; and finally of a group of didactic compositions, long and short, several of which are devoted to a description of the process of learning the scribal art and of the advantages which flow from it.[14]

Some adequate idea of the scope and quantity of Sumerian literature may be obtained from the contents of a hitherto altogether unknown tablet in the Nippur collection of the University Museum which I had the good fortune to identify and decipher in the course of the past year. This tablet is not a literary composition; it is a literary catalogue. That is, it lists by title *one* group of Sumerian literary compositions. The scribe who compiled this list was one of those very scribes of approximately 2000 B. C. who wrote or copied our Sumerian literary tablets; the catalogue, therefore, is contemporaneous with the compositions which it lists. His purpose in compiling the catalogue was no doubt practical. For as is now clear, by approximately 2000 B. C. a large number of literary compositions of all types and sizes were current in Sumer, inscribed on tablets of all shapes and dimensions which had to be handled, stored, and cared for. Some of the scribes in charge of the tablets in the temple or palace "tablet house," therefore, found it convenient to note and list the names of this or that group of literary compositions for purposes of reference essential to the storing and filing of the respective tablets.

The catalogue tablet is in almost perfect condition.[g] It is quite small, 2½ inches in length and 1½ inches in width. Small as it is, the scribe, by dividing each side into two columns and by using a minute script, succeeded in cataloguing the titles of sixty-two Sumerian literary compositions. The first forty titles he divided into groups of ten by ruling a dividing line between numbers 10 and 11, 20 and 21, 30 and 31, 40 and 41. The remaining twenty-two titles he divided into two unequal groups, the first consisting of nine, and the second, of thirteen titles. And what is most interesting, at least twenty-one of the titles which this scribe listed in his catalogue are of compositions whose actual contents we can now reconstruct in large part. Needless to say, we probably have the actual texts of many more compositions whose titles are listed in our Nippur catalogue. But since the title of a

---

FIG. 1. THE ORIGIN AND DEVELOPMENT OF THE SUMERIAN SYSTEM OF WRITING

The cuneiform system [17] of writing was probably originated by the Sumerians. The oldest inscriptions unearthed to date—over one thousand tablets and fragments from the latter half of the fourth millennium B. C. which were excavated in Erech in very recent years—are in all likelihood written in the Sumerian language. But whether or not it was the Sumerians who invented the script, it was certainly they who in the course of the third millennium B. C. fashioned it into an effective writing tool. Its practical value was gradually recognized by the surrounding peoples, who borrowed it from the Sumerians and adapted it to their own languages. By the second millennium B. C. it was current all over the Near East.

The cuneiform script began as pictographic writing; each sign was a picture of one or more concrete objects and represented a word whose meaning was identical with, or closely related to, the object pictured. The defects of a system of this type are obvious; the complicated form of the signs and the huge number of signs required, render it too unwieldy for practical use. The Sumerian scribes overcame the first difficulty by gradually simplifying and conventionalizing the form of the signs until their pictographic origin was no longer apparent. As for the second difficulty, they reduced the number of signs and kept it within effective limits by resorting to various helpful devices. The most significant of these consisted of substituting phonetic for ideographic values. The table on the opposite page was prepared for the purpose of illustrating this two-fold development in the course of the centuries; a detailed description will be found in note 18.

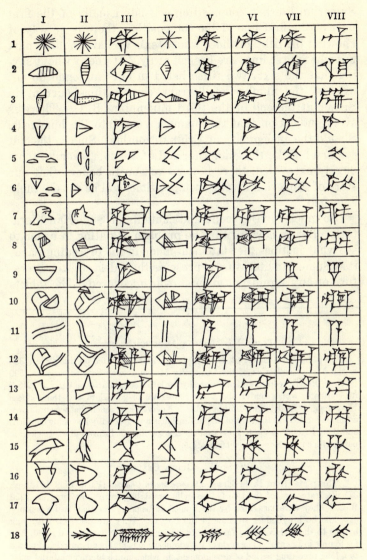

FIG. 1. THE ORIGIN AND DEVELOPMENT OF THE SUMERIAN
SYSTEM OF WRITING

(For description, see opposite page and note 18.)

Sumerian literary composition consists usually of the first part of the first line of the composition, there is no way of knowing the titles of those whose texts we have in large part but whose first lines are broken away. It goes without saying that the sixty-two titles listed in our catalogue do not exhaust the number of literary compositions current in Sumer at the end of the third millennium B. C. There is every indication that this number runs into the hundreds. Should the ancient city of Eridu in southern Sumer, the cult center of Enki, the Sumerian god of wisdom, ever be thoroughly excavated, there is good reason to believe that our store of Sumerian literary compositions will be considerably enlarged.[16]

So much for the scope and contents of Sumerian literature. Let us now turn to the problem of dating in order to see what justifies the statement made in the preceding pages that Sumerian literature represents the oldest written literature of any significant amount ever uncovered. The tablets

---

PLATE III. NIPPUR ARCHAIC CYLINDER

To judge from the script, the Nippur cylinder illustrated on this plate (8383 in the Nippur collection of the University Museum) may date as early as 2500 B. C. Although copied and published by the late George Barton as early as 1918,[20] its contents, which center about the Sumerian air-god Enlil and the goddess Ninhursag, are still largely unintelligible. Nevertheless, much that was unknown or misunderstood at the time of its publication is now gradually becoming clarified, and there is good reason to hope that the not too distant future will see the better part of its contents ready for translation.

PLATE IV. GUDEA CYLINDER

This plate (from E. de Sarzec, *Découvertes en Chaldée* (Paris, 1889–1912), pl. 37) illustrates one of the two Gudea cylinders dating from approximately 2250 B. C. They were excavated by the French at Lagash more than half a century ago, and both cylinders are now in the Louvre. They are inscribed with long hymns to the god Ningirsu (another name for the god Ninurta—see p. 80) and his temple in Lagash. The style of the composition is highly advanced and points to a long preceding period of development, in which much literary material must have been composed and written down. The contents of the two Gudea cylinders were carefully copied and translated by the eminent French Assyriologist, Thureau-Dangin, as early as the first decade of our century.[19] The Sumerological advance of the past several decades, however, makes a new translation imperative.

PLATE III

NIPPUR ARCHAIC CYLINDER
(For description, see opposite page.)

PLATE IV

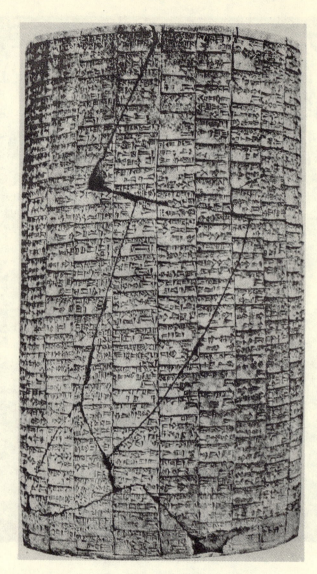

GUDEA CYLINDER

(For description, see page 18.)

themselves, to judge from the script as well as from internal evidence, were inscribed in the Early Post-Sumerian period, the period following immediately upon the fall of the Third Dynasty of Ur. Just as a rough point of reference, therefore, the actual writing of the tablets may be dated approximately 1750 B. C.[a] As for the composition of their contents, to judge from the large group of hymns devoted to the kings of the Third Dynasty of Ur, much of it actually took place in that Neo-Sumerian period which lasted approximately from 2150 to 2050 B. C.[h] Moreover, an analysis of the contents of the hymns inscribed on the so-called Gudea cylinders,[19] which date from approximately 2250 B. C., and of the myth inscribed on an archaic Nippur cylinder published by George Barton,[20] which, to judge from its script, dates considerably earlier than the Gudea cylinders, clearly indicates that not a little of the hymnal and mythological material had already been composed several centuries earlier. Finally, an analysis of the religious concepts as revealed in the building and dedicatory inscriptions of the classical Sumerian period, roughly 2600–2400 B. C., leads to the same conclusion. In short we are amply justified in stating that although practically all our available Sumerian literary tablets actually date from approximately 2000 B. C., a large part of the written literature of the Sumerians was created and developed in the latter half of the third millennium B. C. The fact that so little literary material from these earlier periods has been excavated to date is in large part a matter of archaeological accident. Had it not been, for example, for the Nippur expedition, we would have very little Sumerian literary material from the early post-Sumerian period.

Now let us compare this date with that of the various ancient literatures known to us at present. In Egypt, for example, one might have expected an ancient written literature commensurate with its high cultural development. And, indeed, to judge from the pyramid inscriptions, the Egyptians in all probability did have a well developed written literature in the third millennium B. C. Unfortunately it must have been written largely on papyrus, a readily perishable material, and there is little hope that enough of it will ever be recovered to give a reasonably adequate cross-section of the Egyptian literature of that ancient period. Then, too, there is the hitherto unknown ancient Canaanite literature which has been found inscribed on tablets excavated in the past decade by the French at Rash-esh-Shamra in northern Syria. These tablets, relatively few in number, indicate that the Canaanites, too, had a highly developed literature at one time. They are dated approximately 1400 B. C., that is, they were inscribed over half a millennium *later* than our Sumerian literary tablets.[21] As for the Semitic Babylonian literature as exemplified by such works as the "Epic of Creation," the "Epic of Gilgamesh," etc., it is not only considerably later than our Sumerian literature, but also includes much that is borrowed directly from it.[22]

We turn now to the ancient literatures which have exercised the most profound influence on the more spiritual aspects of our civilization. These are the Bible, which contains the literary creations of the Hebrews; the Iliad and Odyssey, which are filled with the epic and mythic lore of the Greeks; the Rig-veda, which contains the literary products of ancient India; and the Avesta, which contains those of ancient Iran. None of these literary collections were written down in their present form before the first half of the first millennium B. C. Our Sumerian literature, inscribed on tablets dating from approximately 2000 B. C., therefore antedates these literatures by more than a millennium. Moreover, there is another vital difference. The texts of the Bible, of the Iliad and Odyssey, and of the Rig-veda and Avesta, as we have them, have been modified, edited, and redacted by compilers and redactors with varied motives and diverse points of view. Not so our Sumerian literature; it has come down to us as actually inscribed by the ancient scribes of four thousand years ago, unmodified and uncodified by later compilers and commentators.

And so we come to the crucial point. The basic value of Sumerian literature and its fundamental importance for the related humanities being obvious, why has it remained largely unknown; why has it not been made available to scholar and layman? What has hampered and impeded the decipherment of the Sumerian literary tablets? Why has so little progress been made in the reconstruction and translation of their contents? The factors responsible for this unfortunate situation are twofold: *linguistic,* the difficulties presented by the grammar and vocabulary of the Sumerian language; and *textual,* the problems arising out of the physical characteristics of our source material.

First, the linguistic difficulties. Sumerian is neither a Semitic nor an Indo-European language. It belongs to the so-called agglutinative type of languages exemplified by Turkish, Hungarian, and Finnish. None of these languages, however, seems to have any closer affiliation to Sumerian, and the latter, therefore, as yet stands alone and unrelated to any known language living or dead. Its decipherment, therefore, would have been an impossible task, were it not for the fortunate fact already mentioned that the Semitic conquerors of Sumer not only adapted its script to their own Semitic tongue, but also retained it as their literary and religious language. As a consequence, the scribal schools in Babylonia and Assyria made the study of Sumerian their basic discipline. They therefore compiled what may be described as *bilingual* syllabaries or dictionaries in which the Sumerian words or phrases were translated into their own language, Accadian. In addition they also drew up *interlinears* of the Sumerian literary compositions in which each Sumerian line is followed by its Accadian translation. Accadian, being a Semitic tongue related to numerous known languages, was deciphered relatively early. And so these bilinguals became the basic material for the decipherment of Sumerian, for by comparing the known Accadian word or phrase with the corresponding Sumerian, the meaning of the latter could be deduced.

Now while all this sounds relatively simple on paper, in actual practice the decipherment of Sumerian from the bilingual texts has resulted in many grammatical and lexical misunderstandings. For Accadian and Sumerian are as divergent in vocabulary and structure as two languages can be, and the seeming correspondences in the ancient dictionaries and interlinears frequently proved very misleading, especially since not a few of the earlier decipherers, for one reason or another, tended to draw hasty and superficial conclusions. As a consequence so many errors crept into Sumerian grammar and vocabulary that when scholars were presented with some of our *unilingual* literary tablets, that is with the tablets inscribed in Sumerian only, the resulting efforts proved largely unproductive. Indeed in many cases the attempted translations were almost entirely untrustworthy and dangerously misleading. It is only in the last

---

PLATE V. "CHICAGO" SYLLABARY

The dictionaries and syllabaries compiled by the Babylonian scribes to aid their study of the Sumerian language, which formed their basic discipline, varied considerably in make-up and structure. One of the most useful types is the "Chicago" syllabary, a scientific edition of which was recently published by Richard Hallock, of the Oriental Institute.[23] It is illustrated on plate V, which is reproduced here by permission of the University of Chicago Press. It was inscribed in the latter part of the first millennium B. C., although the indications are that it was actually compiled sometime in the second millenium B. C. Each side of the tablet is divided into two halves, and each half is subdivided into four columns. The *second* column contains the cuneiform sign to be explained, while the *third* column gives the name by which the Babylonian scribes identified it. The *first* column writes out phonetically the Sumerian word which the sign represents, while the *fourth* column gives its Semitic translation.

PLATE VI. NIPPUR GRAMMATICAL TEXT

This plate (from Arno Poebel, *Historical and Grammatical Texts* (Philadelphia, 1914), pl. CXXII) illustrates another type of lexical text devised by the Semitic scribes to further their knowledge of Sumerian. It is primarily *grammatical* in character. The tablet originally contained 16 columns. Each column is subdivided into two halves. The left half contains a Sumerian grammatical unit, such as a substantive or verbal complex, while the right half gives its Semitic translation. This tablet is much older than the "Chicago" syllabary; it belongs to the same period as our literary material, approximately 2000 B. C.[24]

PLATE V

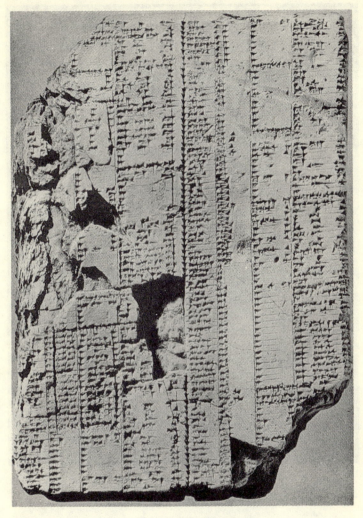

"CHICAGO" SYLLABARY

(For description, see opposite page.)

PLATE VI

NIPPUR GRAMMATICAL TEXT

(For description, see page 22)

two decades, largely as a result of Arno Poebel's *Grund-züge der Sumerischen Grammatik* [25] that Sumerian grammar has been put on a scientific basis. As for the lexical problems, these still remain serious and far from resolved.[26]

But troublesome and distressing as the *linguistic* problems frequently are in the process of reconstructing and translating our literary tablets, they are not insuperable. The major impeding factor, the most serious stumbling block, is the *textual* problem. Tablets, and especially those inscribed with the Sumerian literary compositions which are largely unbaked, rarely come out whole from the ground. Usually they are in a fragmentary, and not infrequently in a *very* fragmentary condition. Offsetting this disadvantage is the happy fact that the ancient scribes made more than one copy of any given composition. The breaks in one tablet may therefore frequently be restored from duplicating pieces which may themselves be mere broken fragments. Thus in the case of "Inanna's Descent to the Nether World" (see p. 83), I utilized fourteen different fragments. In the case of the recently published "Lamentation Over the Destruction of Ur," [15] the text was reconstructed from twenty-two different fragments. And in reconstructing "The Feats and Exploits of Ninurta" (see p. 80), I utilized 49 different fragments. To take full advantage of these duplications and the consequent restorations, however, it is essential to have as much as possible of the source material copied and available. But of the Nippur literary tablets excavated by the University of Pennsylvania and now located in Istanbul and Philadelphia, some *two thousand* in number, only about *five hundred* have been copied and published to date. And while all of the approximately seven hundred pieces in the British Museum, Louvre, Berlin Museum, and Ashmolean Museum have been copied and published,[12] some of the more important texts did not appear until a relatively recent date. Under these circumstances, the trustworthy and scientific reconstruction and translation of our Sumerian literary compositions on any major scale was obviously impossible.

I first realized this situation and its implications in 1933, almost a decade ago, while working in the Oriental Institute of the University of Chicago as a member of its Assyrian Dictionary staff. For in that year died Edward Chiera, the scholar who copied more of the Nippur literary material than all others combined. Long a member of the faculty of the University of Pennsylvania, he devoted much of his time and energy during his stay there to the copying of more than two hundred literary tablets and fragments in the University Musuem. Later, when called to the rapidly expanding Oriental Institute of the University of Chicago as head of its Assyrian Dictionary project, he took his copies with him, and the Oriental Institute undertook to publish them in two volumes. Upon Chiera's untimely death, the editorial department of the Oriental Institute entrusted me with the preparation of these two posthumous volumes for publication.[27] As the significance of the contents dawned upon me, I realized that all efforts to translate and interpret the material would remain scientifically inadequate unless and until more of the uncopied and unpublished material lying in Istanbul and Philadelphia should be made available.

From that day to this I have concentrated all my efforts on the reconstruction and translation of the Sumerian literary compositions. After devoting years to a thorough study of the Sumerian idiom, I travelled to Istanbul in 1937 and spent some twenty months in the Museum of the Ancient Orient, where I copied one hundred and seventy Sumerian literary tablets and fragments from its Nippur collection; unfortunately this still leaves approximately *five hundred* pieces in this Museum uncopied and unavailable. Since returning to the United States in 1939, I have devoted practically all my time and energy to the Sumerian literary tablets and fragments in the Nippur collection of our University Museum. I thus succeeded in identifying approximately *six hundred and seventy-five* uncopied and unpublished Sumerian literary pieces in the collection, almost twice as much as all the literary material copied and published by numerous scholars working in the Museum in the course of the past four decades. Of these six hundred and seventy-five pieces, approximately one hundred and seventy-five are inscribed with epic and mythological material; some three hundred are hymnal in character; fifty are parts of lamentations; the remaining one hundred and fifty are inscribed with proverbs and "wisdom" compositions.

In the past two years my efforts were concentrated largely on the epics and myths. By utilizing all the available published material, together with that part of the unpublished material which I copied in the Museum of the Ancient Orient at Istanbul and all the relevant unpublished material in the University Museum at Philadelphia, I succeeded in reconstructing the larger parts of the texts of twenty-four Sumerian epics and myths; [28] this is the basic source material for the restoration of Sumerian mythology to be sketched in the following chapters. As for the scientific edition of these epics and myths, that is, editions consisting of the reconstructed Sumerian texts with line by line translations and commentary, these are now in the process of preparation; unless the work is unexpectedly interrupted, they should be completed in the course of the coming two or three years.

CHAPTER I

THE SCOPE AND SIGNIFICANCE OF SUMERIAN MYTHOLOGY

The science of comparative mythology, like almost all the sciences, exact and inexact, is largely a product of the nineteenth century; its origin and development followed closely upon that of comparative philology, the science devoted to language and literature. The phenomenal growth of comparative philology itself was due primarily to the recognition that both Sanskrit, the language of the oldest sacred literature of the Hindu peoples, as well as Zend, or Old Persian, the language of the oldest sacred literature of the Iranian peoples, were Indo-European lanuages; that is, they belong to the same family of languages as Greek and Latin. The intense revival of Indo-European philology that followed was therefore based largely on the ancient literatures of the Greeks, Hindus, and Iranians, and this led naturally and directly to a comparative study of the myths and legends as related and revealed in them.

Moreover, toward the end of the first half of the nineteenth century, a new and unexpected field of study was opened to comparative mythology. For it was about this time that the Egyptian hieroglyphic script and the Babylonian cuneiform script were deciphered, and much new mythological material was gradually recovered. What added impetus and excitement to this field of research was the fact that it offered a more scientific approach to the study of the Old Testament. For it soon became evident that some of the Old Testament material was mythological in character, since it presented clear parallels and resemblances to the myths recovered from Egyptian and Babylonian sources. And so the study of comparative mythology, following in the footsteps of philology and linguistics, was no longer restricted to the ancient Indo-Europeans; it now included the ancient Semites and Egyptians.

Approximately at the same time, the growth and development of an almost entirely new science, that of anthropology, proved of fundamental significance for the study of comparative mythology. In all the continents outside of Europe, new peoples and tribes, in various stages of civilization, were being discovered. Students and travellers, scientists and missionaries, studied the new languages, described the strange habits and customs, and wrote down the religious beliefs and practices. Much hitherto unknown mythological material was thus recovered from these more or less primitive peoples, and the science of comparative mythology broadened and expanded accordingly.

And so, roughly speaking, we may divide the source material utilized by comparative mythology into two categories. The first consists of the myths and legends of the ancient cultures such as those of the Hindus, Iranians, and Greeks on the one hand, and of the Hebrews, Babylonians, and Egyptians, on the other; these are revealed in, and derived from, the literatures of these peoples as written down largely in the first millennium B. C. In this group, too, we may class such mythologies as the Scandinavian or Eddic, the Chinese, Japanese, etc., which are derived from literary remains of a much later date. The second category consists of the myths and legends of the so-called primitive peoples discovered in recent centuries, as obtained by word of mouth from living members of those peoples and reported by travellers, missionaries, and anthropologists. It goes without saying that basically, and in the long run, the recent, primitive source material is every bit as important and valuable for comparative mythology and the related sciences as that of the ancient cultures. On the other hand it is quite as obvious that for the history of the progress of our civilization as we see and know it today, it is the tone and temper, the word and spirit of the ancient mythologies, those of the Greeks and Hebrews, of the Hindus and Iranians, of the Babylonians and Egyptians, which are of prime significance. It is the spiritual and religious concepts revealed in these ancient literatures which permeate the modern civilized world.

Still almost entirely unknown to this very moment is Sumerian mythology, the sacred stories of the non-Semitic, non-Indo-European people which in historical times, from approximately 3500 to 2000 B. C., inhabited Sumer, the relatively small land situated between the Tigris and Euphrates Rivers and stretching from the Persian Gulf northward approximately as far as modern Bagdad; a land that may be aptly described as the culture cradle of the entire Near East. Should the reader turn, for example, to Hastings' *Encyclopedia of Religion and Ethics*,[29] and examine the very long article on the cosmogonic or creation myths of the world, he will find a large and relatively exhaustive list of peoples, ancient and modern, cultured and primitive, whose cosmogonic concepts are described and analyzed. But he will look in vain for Sumerian cosmogony. Similarly, the collection entitled *Mythology of All the Races*[30] devotes thirteen volumes to an analysis of the more important mythologies in the world; here, too, however, there will be found few traces of Sumerian mythology. Whatever little is known of Sumerian mythology is largely surmised from the modified, redacted, and in a sense, garbled versions of the Babylonians who conquered the Sumerians toward the very end of the third millennium B. C., and who used the Sumerian stories and legends as a basis and nucleus for the development of their own myths.

But it is a known fact that in the long stretch of time between approximately 3500 and 2000 B. C. it was the Sumerians who represented the dominant cultural group of the entire Near East. It was the Sumerians who developed and probably invented the cuneiform system of writing; who developed a well integrated pantheon together with spiritual and religious concepts which influenced profoundly all the peoples of the Near East; who, finally, created and developed a literature rich in content and effective in form. Moreover, the following significant fact must be borne in mind. By the end of the third millennium B. C. Sumer had already ceased to exist as a political entity and Sumerian had already become a dead language, for by that time Sumer had been overrun and conquered by the Semites, and it is the Semitic Accadian language which gradually became the living, spoken tongue of the land. Nevertheless Sumerian continued to be used as the literary and religious language of the Semitic conquerors for many centuries to come, like Greek in the Roman period and like Latin in the Middle Ages. Indeed for many centuries the study of the Sumerian language and literature remained the basic pursuit of the scribal schools and intellectual and spiritual centers not only of the Babylonians and Assyrians, but also of the many surrounding peoples such as the Elamites, Hurrians, Hittites, and Canaanites. Obviously, then, both because of their content as well as because of their age, the Sumerian mythological tales and concepts must have penetrated and permeated those of the entire Near East. A knowledge of the Sumerian myths and legends is therefore a prime and basic essential for a proper approach to a scientific study of the mythologies current in the ancient Near East, for it illuminates and clarifies to no small extent the background behind their origin and development.[i]

It is this practically unknown Sumerian mythology which I have the privilege of sketching briefly in the pages to follow. The sketch will begin with the myths centering about the creation and organization of the universe and the creation of man. It will continue with the myths of Kur, consisting of three versions of a dragon-slaying motif and of the poem "Inanna's Descent to the Nether World." It will conclude with an outline of three interesting miscellaneous myths. All in all, therefore, it is hoped that the reader will obtain a fairly adequate cross-section of Sumerian mythology, a cross-section which, considering the age of the culture involved, is remarkably broad in scope and surprisingly full in detail.

CHAPTER II

MYTHS OF ORIGINS *

The most significant myths of a given culture are usually the cosmogonic, or creation myths, the sacred stories evolved and developed in an effort to explain the origin of the universe, the presence of the gods, and the existence of man. And so we shall devote this chapter, by far the longest in our monograph, to the creation theories and concepts current in Sumer in the third millennium B. C. The subject lends itself to treatment under three heads: (1) the creation of the universe, (2) the organization of the universe, (3) the creation of man.

THE CREATION OF THE UNIVERSE

The major source for the Sumerian conception of the creation of the universe is the introductory passage to a Sumerian poem which I have entitled "Gilgamesh, Enkidu, and the Nether World." The history of its decipherment is illuminating and not uninteresting. In 1934, when I first tried to decipher the contents, I found that eight pieces belonging to the poem—seven excavated in Nippur and one in Ur—had already been copied and published, thus: Hugo Radau, once of the University Museum, published two from Philadelphia in 1910; Stephen Langdon published two from Istanbul in 1914; Edward Chiera published one from Istanbul in 1924 and two more from Philadelphia in 1934; C. J. Gadd, of the British Museum, published an excellently preserved tablet from Ur in 1930.[32] But an intelligent recon-

* In the translated Sumerian passages italics indicate doubtful renderings as well as foreign words. Words between parentheses are not in the Sumerian text but are added for purposes of clarification. Words between brackets are broken away and lost from the original, and are supplied by the author. Words between quotation marks represent literal translations of Sumerian words whose fuller implications are too uncertain to permit a more idiomatic rendering.

struction and translation of the myth were still impossible, largely because the tablets and fragments, some of which seemed to duplicate each other without rhyme or reason and with but little variation in their wording, could not be properly arranged. In 1936, after I had sent off to the *Revue d'assyriologie* my first translations of the myth "Inanna's Descent to the Nether World" (see p. 83), I decided to make a serious effort to reconstruct the contents of the poem, which obviously seemed to contain a charming and significant story. And it was then that I came upon the clue which enabled me to arrange the pieces in their proper order.

This clue crystallized from an effective utilization of two stylistic features which characterize Sumerian poetry. The first is one which ranks very low in the scale of artistic technique but which from the point of view of the decipherer is truly a boon. It may be described as follows. When the poet finds it advisable to repeat a given description or incident, he makes this repeated passage coincide with the original to the very last detail. Thus when a god or hero orders his messenger to deliver a message, this message, no matter how long and detailed, is given twice in the text, first when the messenger is instructed by his master, and a second time when the message is actually delivered. The two versions are thus practically identical, and the breaks in the one passage may be restored from the other.

As for the second stylistic feature, it may be thus sketched. The Sumerian poet uses *two* dialects in his epic and mythic compositions, the *main* dialect, and another known as the *Emesal* dialect. The latter resembles the main dialect very closely and differs only in showing several regular and characteristic phonetic variations. What is more interesting, however, is the fact that the poet uses this Emesal dialect in rendering the direct speech of a *female,* not male, deity; thus the speeches of Inanna, queen of heaven, are regularly rendered in the Emesal dialect.[33] And so, on examining carefully the texts before me, I realized that what in the case of several passages had been taken to be a mere meaningless and unmotivated duplication, actually contained a speech of the goddess Inanna in which she repeats in the *Emesal* dialect all that the poet had previously described in narrative form in the *main* dialect. With

---

PLATE VII. GODS AND THE NETHER WORLD

One of the more remarkable contributions to art made by Mesopotamia is the cylinder seal. Invented primarily for the purpose of identifying and safeguarding ownership of goods shipped or stored, it came to be used in time as a kind of signature for legal documents. The procedure consisted merely of rolling the cylinder over wet clay and thus impressing the seal's design upon it. It is the contents of these designs engraved by the seal-cutters on the stone cylinders which are of considerable value for our study of Sumerian mythology. Especially is this true of the cylinder seals current in Sumer in the latter half of the third millennium B. C., not a few of whose designs are religious and mythological in character.[31]

The upper design clearly attempts to portray a more or less complicated mythological story. Three of the deities can be identified with reasonable certainty. Second from the right is the water-god Enki, with the flowing streams of water and the swimming fishes. Immediately behind him is his Janus-faced messenger Isimud, who plays an important role in several of our Enki myths. Seemingly rising out of the lower regions is Utu, the sun-god, with his saw-knife and fiery rays. The female figure standing on top of the mountain, near what seems to be a rather desolate tree, may perhaps be Inanna. If the figure to the left with bow in hand is intended to be Gilgamesh, we have in this design most of the protagonists of the tale "Gilgamesh, Enkidu, and the Nether World." However, it is to be noted that Enkidu is missing, and Isimud, who is pictured in the design, plays no part in the story. And so any close connection between the design and the epic tale is improbable.

In the central design none of the figures can be identified with reasonable certainty. In the left half of the picture we note a deity who seems to be rising out of the lower regions and is presenting a macelike object to a goddess. To the left is a god, perhaps Gilgamesh, who seems to be chopping down a tree whose trunk is bent to a curve. The right half of the design seems to depict a ritual scene.

The lower design may illustrate graphically the meaning of such a phrase as, "The nether world has seized him" (see p. 35). In the right half of the scene we note a god actually within a flaming mountain (in Sumerian the word meaning "mountain" is the word used regularly for "nether world"). To the right of the mountain is a god who may be putting it to flame with a torch. Behind this deity is a goddess with fiery rays and ring who may perhaps be identified as Inanna. The left half of the design portrays a god holding a bull-man by the tail; both are inside a mountain.

(Reproduced, by permission of the Macmillan Company, from Henri Frankfort, *Cylinder Seals* (London, 1939), plates XIXa, XXIa, and XVIIIj.)

PLATE VII

GODS AND THE NETHER WORLD
(For description, see opposite page.)

this clue as a guide I succeeded in piecing together the first part of this poem; this was published in 1938.[34]   The latter half of the poem still remained largely unintelligible, and even the first and published part had several serious breaks in the text.   In 1939 I found in Istanbul a broken prism inscribed with the poem.   And in the course of the past year I identified and copied 7 additional pieces in the University Museum at Philadelphia.[35]   As a result we now have 16 pieces inscribed with the poem; over two hundred and fifty lines of its text can now be intelligently reconstructed and, barring a passage here and there, be correctly translated.

The story of our poem, briefly sketched, runs as follows: Once upon a time there was a *huluppu*-tree, perhaps a willow; it was planted on the banks of the Euphrates; it was nurtured by the waters of the Euphrates.   But the South Wind tore at it, root and crown, while the Euphrates flooded it with its waters.   Inanna, queen of heaven, walking by, took the tree in her hand and brought it to Erech, the seat of her main sanctuary, and planted it in her holy garden. There she tended it most carefully.   For when the tree grew big, she planned to make of its wood a chair for herself and a couch.

Years passed, the tree matured and grew big.   But Inanna found herself unable to cut down the tree.   For at its base the snake "who knows no charm" had built its nest.   In its crown, the Zu-bird—a mythological creature which at times wrought mischief—had placed its young. In the middle Lilith, the maid of desolation, had built her house.   And so poor Inanna, the light-hearted and ever joyful maid, shed bitter tears.   And as the dawn broke and her brother, the sun-god Utu, arose from his sleeping chamber, she repeated to him tearfully all that had befallen her *huluppu*-tree.

Now Gilgamesh, the great Sumerian hero, the forerunner of the Greek Heracles, who lived in Erech, overheard Inanna's weeping complaint and chivalrously came to her rescue.   He donned his armour weighing fifty minas—about fifty pounds—and with his "ax of the road," seven talents and seven minas in weight—over four hundred pounds—he slew the snake "who knows no charm" at the base of the tree. Seeing which, the Zu-Bird fled with his young to the mountain, and Lilith tore down her house and fled to the desolate places which she was accustomed to haunt. The men of Erech who had accompanied Gilgamesh now cut down the tree and presented it to Inanna for her chair and couch.

What did Inanna do? Of the base of the *huluppu*-tree she made an object called the *pukku* (probably a drum), and of its crown she made another related object called the *mikku* (probably a drumstick), and gave them both to Gilgamesh, evidently as a reward for his gallantry. Follows a passage of twelve lines describing Gilgamesh's activity with these two objects whose meaning I am still unable to penetrate, although it is in perfect shape. When our story becomes intelligible again, it continues with the statement that "because of the cry of the young maidens" the *pukku* and the *mikku* fell into the nether world, evidently through a hole in the ground. Gilgamesh put in his hand to retrieve them but was unable to reach them; he put in his foot but was quite as unsuccessful. And so he seated himself at the gate of the nether world and cried with fallen face:[j]

> My *pukku*, who will bring it up from the nether world?
> My *mikku*, who will bring it up from the "face" of the nether world?

His servant, Enkidu, his constant follower and companion, heard his master's cries, and said to him:

> My master, why dost thou cry, why is thy heart sick?
> Thy *pukku*, I will bring it up from the nether world,
> Thy *mikku*, I will bring it up from the "face" of the nether world.

Thereupon Gilgamesh warned him of the dangers involved in his plan to descend to the nether world—a splendid passage, brief and concise in describing the taboos of the lower regions. Said Gilgamesh to Enkidu:

If now thou wilt descend to the nether world,
A word I speak to thee, take my word,
Advice I offer thee, take my advice.

Do not put on clean clothes,
Lest the (*dead*) *heroes* will come forth like enemies;
Do not anoint thyself with the good oil of the vessel,
Lest at its smell they will crowd about thee.

Do not throw the throw-stick in the nether world,
Lest they who were struck down by the throw-stick will sur-
    round thee;
Do not carry a staff in thy hand,
Lest the shades will flutter all about thee.

Do not put sandals on thy feet,
In the nether world make no cry;
Kiss not thy beloved wife,
Kiss not thy beloved son,
Strike not thy hated wife,
Strike not thy hated son,
Lest thy "cry" of the nether world will seize thee;
(*The cry*) *for* her who is lying, for her who is lying,
The mother of the god Ninazu who is lying,
Whose holy body no garment covers,
Whose holy breast no cloth wraps.

But Enkidu heeded not the advice of his master and he
did the very things against which Gilgamesh had warned
him. And so he was seized by the nether world and was unable to reascend to the earth. Thereupon Gilgamesh,
greatly troubled, proceeded to the city of Nippur and wept
before the great air-god Enlil, the god who in the third millennium B. C. was the leading deity of the Sumerian pantheon:

O Father Enlil, my *pukku* fell into the nether world,
My *mikku* fell into the nether world;
I sent Enkidu to bring them up to me, the nether world has
    seized him.
Namtar (a demon) has not seized him, Ashak (a demon) has not
    seized him,
    The nether world has seized him.
Nergal, the ambusher, who spares no one, has not seized him,
    The nether world has seized him.
In battles where heroism is displayed he has not fallen,
    The nether world has seized him.

But Enlil refused to stand by Gilgamesh, who then proceeded to Eridu and repeated his plea before the water-god Enki, the "god of wisdom." Enki ordered the sun-god Utu to open a hole in the nether world and to allow the shade of Enkidu to ascend to earth. The sun-god Utu did as bidden and the shade of Enkidu appeared to Gilgamesh. Master and servant embraced and Gilgamesh questioned Enkidu about what he saw in the nether world. The passage from here to the end of the poem is badly broken, but the following partly extant colloquy will serve as an illustration:[k]

> *Gilgamesh:* "Him who has one son hast thou seen?"
> *Enkidu:* "I have seen."
> *Gilgamesh:* "How is he treated?"
> *Enkidu:* (Answer broken)
>
> *Gilgamesh:* "Him who has two sons hast thou seen?"
> *Enkidu:* "I have seen."
> *Gilgamesh:* "How is he treated?"
> *Enkidu:* (Answer broken)
>
> *Gilgamesh:* "Him who has three sons hast thou seen?"
> *Enkidu:* "I have seen."
> *Gilgamesh:* "How is he treated?"
> *Enkidu:* ". . . much water he drinks."

PLATE VIII. THE SEPARATION OF HEAVEN AND EARTH

The two pieces illustrated here are duplicates belonging to the epic tale, "Gilgamesh, Enkidu, and the Nether World." The one to the left is a tablet (14068 in the Nippur collection of the University Museum) published by Chiera in 1934.[36] The one to the right (4429 in the Nippur collection of the Museum of the Ancient Orient at Istanbul) is a fragment of a prism copied by the author and hitherto unpublished. The marked passages contain the lines significant for the creation of the universe; for the translation and the transliteration, see page 37 and note 37.

PLATE IX. ENLIL SEPARATES HEAVEN AND EARTH

The tablet (13877 in the Nippur collection of the University Museum) illustrated [38] here is one of the 20 duplicating pieces utilized to reconstruct the text of the poem, "The Creation of the Pickax" (see p. 51). Its first five lines are significant for the Sumerian concepts of the creation of the universe; for the translation and the transliteration, see page 40 and note 39.

PLATE VIII

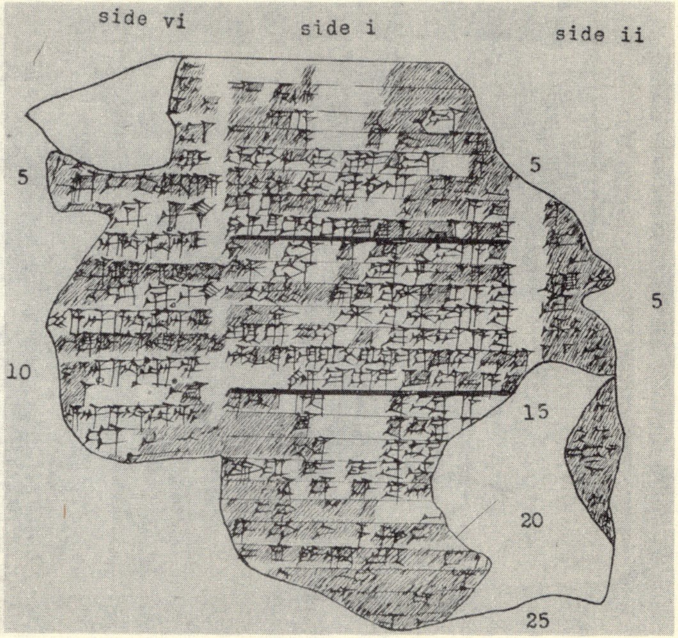

THE SEPARATION OF HEAVEN AND EARTH
(For description, see opposite page.)

PLATE IX

Enlil Separates Heaven and Earth

(For description, see page 36.)

Gilgamesh: "Him who has four sons hast thou seen?"
Enkidu: "I have seen."
Gilgamesh: "How is he treated?"
Enkidu: "Like . . . his heart rejoices."

Gilgamesh: "Him who has five sons hast thou seen?"
Enkidu: "I have seen."
Gilgamesh: "How is he treated?"
Enkidu: "Like a good scribe, his *arm* has been opened,
   He brings justice to the palace."

Gilgamesh: "Him who has six sons hast thou seen?"
Enkidu: "I have seen."
Gilgamesh: "How is he treated?"
Enkidu: "Like him who *guides* the plow his heart rejoices."

Gilgamesh: "Him who has seven sons hast thou seen?"
Enkidu: "I have seen."
Gilgamesh: "How is he treated?"
Enkidu: "As one close to the gods, he . . ."

Another of the questions runs thus:

Gilgamesh: "Him whose dead body lies (unburied) in the plain hast
   thou seen?"
Enkidu: "I have seen."
Gilgamesh: "How is he treated?"
Enkidu: "His shade finds no rest in the nether world." [1]

And so our poem ends.[40] It is the *introduction* to this
composition which furnishes the most significant material
for the Sumerian concepts of the creation of the universe.
The intelligible part of the introduction reads as follows:

After heaven had been moved away from earth,
After earth had been separated from heaven,
After the name of man had been fixed;

After An had carried off heaven,
After Enlil had carried off earth,
After Ereshkigal had been carried off into Kur as its prize;

After he had set sail, after he had set sail,
After the father for Kur had set sail,
After Enki for Kur had set sail;

Against the king the small ones it (Kur) hurled,
Against Enki, the large ones it hurled;
Its small ones, stones of the hand,
Its large ones, stones of . . . reeds,
The keel of the boat of Enki,
In battle, like the attacking storm, overwhelm;

Against the king, the water at the head of the boat,
Like a wolf devours,
Against Enki, the water at the rear of the boat,
Like a lion strikes down.

If we paraphrase and analyze the contents of this passage, it may be worded as follows: Heaven and earth, originally united, were separated and moved away from each other, and thereupon the creation of man was ordained. An, the heaven-god, then carried off heaven, while Enlil, the air-god, carried off earth. All this seems to be according to plan. Then, however, occurred something disruptive. For the goddess Ereshkigal, the counterpart of the Greek Persephone, whom we know as queen of the nether world, but who originally was probably a sky-goddess, was carried off into the nether world, perhaps by Kur. No doubt to avenge this deed, the water-god Enki set sail to attack Kur. The latter, evidently to be conceived as a monster or dragon, did not stand idly by, but hurled stones, large and small, against the keel of Enki's boat, while the primeval waters attacked Enki's boat front and rear. Our poem does not give the result of this struggle between Enki and Kur, since the entire cosmogonic or creation introduction has nothing to do with the basic contents of our Gilgamesh composition; it was placed at the head of the poem only because the Sumerian scribes were accustomed to begin their stories with several introductory lines dealing with creation.

It is from the first half of this introduction that we obtain therefore the following cosmogonic concepts:

1. At one time heaven and earth were united.
2. Some of the gods existed before the separation of heaven and earth.

3. Upon the separation of heaven and earth, it was, as might have been expected, the heaven-god An who carried off heaven, but it was the air-god Enlil who carried off the earth.

Among the crucial points *not stated or implied* in this passage are the following:

1. Were heaven and earth conceived as created, and if so, by whom?
2. What was the shape of heaven and earth as conceived by the Sumerians?
3. Who separated heaven from earth?

Fortunately, the answers to these three questions can be gleaned from several other Sumerian texts dating from our period. Thus:

1. In a tablet which gives a list of the Sumerian gods,[41] the goddess Nammu, written with the ideogram for "sea," is described as "the mother, who gave birth to heaven and earth." Heaven and earth were therefore conceived by the Sumerians as the created products of the primeval sea.
2. The myth "Cattle and Grain" (see p. 53), which describes the birth in heaven of the spirits of cattle and grain, who were then sent down to earth to bring prosperity to mankind, begins with the following two lines:

> After on the mountain of heaven and earth,
> An had caused the Anunnaki (his followers) to be born, . . .

It is not unreasonable to assume, therefore, that heaven and earth united were conceived as a mountain whose base was the bottom of the earth and whose peak was the top of the heaven.
3. The myth "The Creation of the Pickax" (see p. 51), which describes the fashioning and dedication of this valuable agricultural implement, is introduced with the following passage:

> The lord, that which is *appropriate* verily he caused to appear,
> The lord whose decisions are unalterable,
> Enlil, who brings up the seed of the land from the earth,
> *Took care* to move away heaven from earth,
> *Took care* to move away earth from heaven.

And so we have the answer to our third question; it was the air-god Enlil, who separated and removed heaven from earth.

If now we sum up the cosmogonic or creation concepts of the Sumerians, evolved to explain the origin of the universe, they may be stated as follows:

1. First was the *primeval sea*. Nothing is said of its origin or birth, and it is not unlikely that the Sumerians conceived it as having existed eternally.

2. The *primeval sea* begot the cosmic *mountain* consisting of heaven and earth united.

3. Conceived as gods in human form, An (heaven) was the male and Ki (earth) was the female. From their union was begotten the air-god Enlil.

PLATE X. MISCELLANEOUS MYTHOLOGICAL SCENES

The upper design depicts the rising of Utu, the sun-god, identifiable by his fiery rays and saw-knife. He places his left foot on a mountain while attending deities throw open the gates.

In the second design two of the deities are identifiable. At the extreme right is Enki, the water-god, enthroned in his "sea house," perhaps the very house described in "Enki and Eridu" (see p. 62). To the left of the center is Utu, the sun-god, with fiery rays and saw-knife. He stands with one foot on a winged lion while the other steps on a crouching deity. The kneeling figure at the left, holding a gatepost, is probably an attendant of Enki. The deity between Utu and Enki, who is climbing a mountain, is still unidentifiable.

The third design depicts an unidentified god with fiery rays, travelling in his boat; the scene is reminiscent of Nanna's journey to Nippur (see p. 47). The stern of the boat ends in the head of a snake, while the prow ends in the body of a god who is working a punting pole. In the boat are various pots, agricultural implements, and a human-headed lion. On the shore is a vegetation goddess, perhaps to be identified as Uttu, the goddess of plants (see p. 57), or Ashnan, the goddess of grain (see p. 53).

The lower design depicts what is probably a divine connubium.

(Reproduced, by permission of the Macmillan Company, from Henri Frankfort, *Cylinder Seals*, plates XVIIIa, k, XIXe, and XVI.)

PLATE X

MISCELLANEOUS MYTHOLOGICAL SCENES

(For description, see opposite page.)

4. Enlil, the air-god, separated heaven from earth, and while his father An carried off heaven, Enlil himself carried off his mother Ki, the earth. The union of Enlil and his mother Ki—in historical times she is perhaps to be identified with the goddess called variously Ninmah, "great queen"; Ninhursag, "queen of the (cosmic) mountain"; Nintu, "queen who gives birth"—set the stage for the organization of the universe, the creation of man, and the establishment of civilization.[42]

THE ORGANIZATION OF THE UNIVERSE

The Sumerian expression for "universe" is *an-ki*, literally "heaven-earth." The organization of the universe may therefore be subdivided into that of heaven and that of earth. Heaven consists of the sky and the space above the sky which is called the "great above"; here dwell the sky-gods. Earth consists of the surface of the earth and the space below which is called the "great below"; here dwell the underworld or chthonic deities. For the organization of heaven the relatively little mythological material which is available to date may be sketched as follows: Nanna, the moon-god, the major astral deity of the Sumerians, is born of Enlil, the air-god, and his wife Ninlil, the air-goddess. Nanna, the moon-god, is conceived as travelling in a gufa across the heavens, thus bringing light to the pitch-dark lapis lazuli sky. The "little ones," the stars, are scattered about him like grain while the "big ones," perhaps the planets, walk about him like wild oxen." [43]

Nanna, the moon-god, and his wife Ningal are the parents of Utu, the sun-god, who rises in the "mountain of the east" and sets in the "mountain of the west." As yet we find no mention of any boat or chariot used by the sun-god Utu to traverse the sky. Nor is it clear just what he does at night.[m] The not unnatural assumption that upon reaching the "mountain of the west" at the end of the day he continues his journey at night through the nether world, arriving at the "mountain of the east" at dawn, is not borne out by the extant data. Indeed to judge from a prayer to the sun-god which reads: [44]

> O Utu, shepherd of the land, father of the black-headed people,
> When thou liest down, the people, too, lie down,
> O hero Utu, when thou risest, the people, too, rise.

or from a description of the break of dawn which reads: [45]

> As light broke forth, as the horizon grew bright, . . .
> As Utu came forth from his *ganunu,*

or from a description of the setting of the sun which reads: [46]

> Utu has gone forth with lifted head to the bosom of his mother Ningal;

the Sumerians seemed to have conceived of Utu as sleeping through the night.

Turning to the organization of the earth, we learn that it was Enlil, the air-god, who "caused the good day to come forth"; who set his mind to "bring forth seed from the earth" and to establish the *hegal,* that is, plenty, abundance, and prosperity in the land. It was this same Enlil who fashioned the pickax and probably the plow as prototypes of the agricultural implements to be used by man; who appointed Enten, the farmer-god, as his steadfast and trustworthy field-worker. On the other hand it was the water-god Enki who begot Uttu, the goddess of plants. It is Enki, moreover, who actually organizes the earth, and especially that part of it which includes Sumer and its surrounding neighbors, into a going concern. He decrees the fates of Sumer, Ur, and Meluhha, and appoints the various minor deities to their specific duties. And it is both Enlil and Enki, that is, both the air-god and the water-god, who send Lahar, the cattle-god, and Ashnan, the grain-goddess, from heaven to earth in order to make abundant its cattle and grain.

The above outline of the organization of the universe is based upon nine Sumerian myths whose contents we now have wholly or in large part. Two of these involve the moon-god Nanna; they are: *Enlil and Ninlil: the Begetting of Nanna; The Journey of Nanna to Nippur.* The remaining seven are of prime importance for the Sumerian concepts of the origin and establishment of culture and civilization on earth. These are *Emesh and Enten: Enlil Chooses the Farmer-god; The Creation of the Pickax; Cattle and Grain; Enki and Ninhursag: the Affairs of the Water-god; Enki and Sumer: the Organization of the Earth and its Cultural Processes; Enki and Eridu: the Journey of the Water-god to Nippur; Inanna and Enki: the Transfer of the Arts of Civilization from Eridu to Erech.* We shall now proceed to sketch briefly the contents of each of these myths; their wealth and variety, it is hoped, will enable the reader to evaluate the Sumerian mythological concepts together with their spiritual and religious implications.

ENLIL AND NINLIL: THE BEGETTING OF NANNA[n]

This delightful myth, consisting of 152 lines of text,[49] is almost complete. It seems to have been evolved to explain the begetting of the moon-god Nanna as well as that of the three underworld deities, Nergal, Ninazu, and a third whose name is illegible. If rightly interpreted this poem furnishes us with the first known example of the metamorphosis of a god; Enlil assumes the form of three different individuals in impregnating his wife Ninlil with the three nether world deities.

The poem begins with an introductory passage descriptive of the city of Nippur, a Nippur that seems to be conceived as having existed before the creation of man:

> Behold the "bond of heaven and earth," the city, . . .
> Behold Nippur, the city, . . .
> Behold the "kindly wall," the city, . . .
> Behold the Idsalla, its pure river,
> Behold the Karkurunna, its quay,
> Behold the Karasarra, its quay where the boats stand,
> Behold the Pulal, its well of good water,
> Behold the Idnunbirdu, its pure canal,
> Behold Enlil, its young man,
> Behold Ninlil, its young maid,
> Behold Nunbarshegunu, its old woman.

After this brief background sketch the actual story begins. Nunbarshegunu, the "old woman" of Nippur, Ninlil's mother, instructs her daughter how to obtain the love
of Enlil:

> In those days the mother, her begetter, gave advice to the maid,
> Nunbarshegunu gave advice to Ninlil:
> "At the pure river, O maid, at the pure river wash thyself,
> O Ninlil, walk along the bank of the Idnunbirdu,
> The bright-eyed, the lord, the bright-eyed,
> The 'great mountain,' father Enlil, the bright-eyed, will see thee,
> The sheperd . . . who decrees the fates, the bright-eyed, will see
> thee,
> He will . . . , he will kiss thee."

Ninlil follows her mother's instructions and as a consequence is impregnated by "the water" of Enlil and conceives the moon-god Nanna. Enlil then departs from Nippur in the direction of the nether world, but is followed by
Ninlil. As he leaves the gate he instructs the "man of the
gate" to give the inquisitive Ninlil no information of his
whereabouts. Ninlil comes up to the "man of the gate"
and demands to know whither Enlil has gone. *Enlil then*

PLATE XI. ENLIL AND NINLIL: THE BEGETTING OF NANNA

This illustrates the obverse of a tablet (9205 in the Nippur collection of the
University Museum) that was published by the late George Barton as early as
1918.[47] Its contents, though obviously most significant for Sumerian mythology,
have remained largely unintelligible all these years. Sumerological progress in
the course of the past quarter-century and the discovery by the author of nine
additional fragments (eight in the University Museum and one in the Museum
of the Ancient Orient) [48] have now made the reconstruction and translation of
this poem possible. The marked passage contains the following lines:

> ^{d}en-líl-li ì-du ^{d}nin-líl in-uš
> ^{d}nu-nam-nir ì-du ki-sikil mu-un- . . .
> ^{d}en-líl-li lú-ká-gal-ra gù mu-na-dé-e
> lú-ká-gal lú-^{giš}si-gar-ra
> lú-^{giš}šu-di-eš lú-^{giš}si-gar-kug-ga
> nin-zu-^{d}nin-líl-li i-im-du
> u₄-da én-mu mu-ra-tar-ra
> za-e ki-mu nam-mu-ni-in-pàd-dè

For the translation, see page 45.

PLATE XI

ENLIL AND NINLIL: THE BEGETTING OF NANNA

(For description, see opposite page.)

seems to take the form of the "man of the gate" and an-swers for him. The passage involved is as yet unintelligible; it seems to contain a refusal to divulge Enlil's where-abouts. Ninlil thereupon reminds him that while, true enough, Enlil is his king, she is his queen. Thereupon Enlil, still impersonating "the man of the gate," cohabits with her and impregnates her. As a result Ninlil conceives Meslamtaea, more commonly known as Nergal, the king of the nether world. In spite of the unintelligible parts, the flavor of this remarkable passage will be readily apparent from the following quotations:

> Enlil . . . departed from the city,
> Nunamnir (a name of Enlil) . . . departed from the city.
> Enlil walked, Ninlil followed,
> Nunamnir walked, the maid *followed,*
> Enlil says to the man of the gate:

> "O man of the gate, man of the lock,
> O man of the bolt, man of the pure lock,
> Thy queen Ninlil is coming;
> If she asks thee about me,
> Tell her not where I am."

> Ninlil approached the man of the gate:
> "O man of the gate, man of the lock,
> O man of the bolt, man of the pure lock,
> Enlil, thy king, *where is he going?*"

> Enlil answers her *for* the man of the gate:
> "Enlil, the king of all the lands, has commanded me":

Four lines follow containing the substance of this command but their meaning is obscure. Then comes the following dialogue between Ninlil and Enlil, the latter impersonating the "man of the gate":

> *Ninlil:* "True, Enlil is thy king, but I am thy queen."
> *Enlil:* "If now thou art my queen, let my hand touch thy . . ."
> *Ninlil:* "The 'water' of thy king, the bright 'water' is in my heart,
> The 'water' of Nanna, the bright 'water' is in my heart."
> *Enlil:* "The 'water' of my king, let it go toward heaven, let it go to-ward earth,
> Let my 'water,' like the 'water' of my king, go toward earth."

Enlil, *as* the man of the gate, lay down in the . . . ,
He kissed her, he cohabited with her,
Having kissed her, having cohabited with her,
The "water" of . . . Meslamtaea he *caused to flow over* (her)
     heart.

The poem then continues with the begetting of the nether
world deity Ninazu; this time it is the "man of the river of
the nether world, the man-devouring river" whom Enlil
impersonates. In all other respects, the passage is a repe-
tition of that describing the begetting of Meslamtaea; thus:

Enlil walked, Ninlil followed,
Nunamnir walked, the maid *followed,*
Enlil says to the man of the river of the nether world, the man-
     devouring river:

"O man of the river of the nether world, the man-devouring river,
Thy queen Ninlil is coming;
If she asks thee about me,
Tell her not where I am."

Ninlil approached the man of the river of the nether world, the
     man-devouring river:
"O man of the river of the nether world, the man-devouring river,
Enlil, thy king, *where is he going?*"

Enlil answers her *for* the man of the river of the nether world,
     the man-devouring river:
"Enlil, the king of all the lands, has commanded me."

The substance of the command is unintelligible. Follows the dialogue between Ninlil and Enlil, the latter impersonating the "man of the river of the nether world, the man-
devouring river":

Ninlil: "True, Enlil is thy king, but I am thy queen."
Enlil: "If now thou art my queen, let my hand touch thy . . ."
Ninlil: "The 'water' of thy king, the bright 'water' is in my heart,
     The 'water' of Nanna, the bright 'water' is in my heart."
Enlil: "The 'water' of my king, let it go toward heaven, let it go to-
     ward earth,
     Let my 'water,' like the 'water' of my king, go toward earth."
Enlil, *as* the man of the river of the nether world, the man-devouring
     river, lay down in the . . . ,
     He kissed her, he cohabited with her,

Having kissed her, having cohabited with her,
The "water" of Ninazu, the king of . . . , he *caused to flow
over* (her) heart.

The poem then continues with the begetting of the third
underworld deity whose name is illegible; this time it is
the "man of the boat" whom Enlil impersonates. Our
myth then comes to a close with a brief hymnal passage in
which Enlil is exalted as the lord of abundance and the king
whose decrees are unalterable.

THE JOURNEY OF NANNA TO NIPPUR

To the Sumerians of the third millennium B. C., Nippur
was the spiritual center of their country. Its tutelary
deity, Enlil, was the leading god of the Sumerian pantheon;
his temple, Ekur, was the most important temple in Sumer.
And so, the blessing of Enlil was a prime essential for the
establishment of prosperity and abundance in the other
important cities of Sumer, such as Eridu and Ur. To obtain this blessing, the tutelary deities of these cities were
conceived as travelling to Nippur laden with gifts for its
god and temple. Our myth [50] describes just such a journey
from Ur to Nippur of the moon-god Nanna (also known as
Sin and Ashgirbabbar), the tutelary deity of Ur. In this
myth, as in the preceding Enlil-Ninlil composition, the cities
such as Nippur and Ur seem to be fully built and rich in
animal and plant life, although man seems to be still non-
existent.

Beginning with a description of the glory of Nippur, our
poem continues a passage describing Nanna's decision to
visit his father's city:

To go to his city, to stand before his father,
Ashgirbabbar set his mind:
"I, the hero, to my city I would go, before my father I would
stand;
I, Sin, to my city I would go, before my father I would stand,
Before my father Enlil I would stand;
I, to my city I would go, before my mother Ninlil I would stand,
Before my father I would stand."

And so he loads up his gufa with a rich assortment of trees, plants, and animals. On his journey from Ur to Nippur, Nanna and his boat make stop at five cities: Im (?), Larsa, Erech, and two cities whose names are illegible; in each of these Nanna is met and greeted by the respective tutelary deity. Finally he arrives at Nippur:

> At the lapis lazuli quay, the quay of Enlil,
> Nanna-Sin drew up his boat,
> At the white quay, the quay of Enlil,
> Ashgirbabbar drew up his boat,
> On the . . . of the father, his begetter, he stationed himself,
> To the gatekeeper of Enlil he says:

> "Open the house, gatekeeper, open the house,
> Open the house, O protecting genie, open the house,
> Open the house, *thou who makest the trees come forth,* open the house,
> O . . . , *who makest the trees come forth,* open the house,
> Gatekeeper, open the house, O protecting genie, open the house."

He then proceeds to enumerate to the gatekeeper all the gifts which he had brought on his boat, closing with:

> "Gatekeeper, open the house, O protecting genie, open the house,
> That which is at the head of the boat, that which is at the head,
> I would give thee,
> That which is at the rear of the boat, that which is at the rear,
> I would give thee."

The gatekeeper opens the door for Nanna:

> Joyfully, the gatekeeper joyfully opened the door;
> The protecting genie *who makes the trees come forth,* joyfully,
> The gatekeeper joyfully opened the door;
> He *who makes the trees come forth,* joyfully,
> The gatekeeper joyfully opened the door;
> With Sin, Enlil rejoiced.

The two gods feast; then Nanna addresses Enlil his father as follows:

> "In the river give me overflow,
> In the field give me *much* grain,
> In the swampland give me *grass* and *reeds,*
> In the forests give me . . .

> In the plain give me . . .
> In the palm-grove and vineyard give me honey and wine,
> In the palace give me long life,
> To Ur I shall go."

And Enlil accedes to his son's request:

> He gave him, Enlil gave him,
> To Ur he went.
> In the river he gave him overflow,
> In the field he gave him *much* grain,
> In the swampland he gave him *grass* and *reeds,*
> In the forests he gave him . . . ,
> In the plain he gave him . . . ,
> In the palm-grove and vineyard he gave him honey and wine,
> In the palace he gave him long life.

EMESH AND ENTEN: ENLIL CHOOSES THE FARMER–GOD

This myth [51] is the closest extant Sumerian parallel to the Biblical Cain-Abel story, although it ends with a reconciliation rather than a murder. It consists of over three hundred lines, only about half of which are complete; because of the numerous breaks, the meaning of the text is therefore often difficult to penetrate. Tentatively the contents of the poem may be reconstructed as follows:

Enlil, the air-god, has set his mind to bring forth trees and grain and to establish abundance and prosperity in the land. For this purpose two cultural beings, the brothers Emesh and Enten, are created, and Enlil assigns to each specific duties. The text is so badly damaged at this point that it is impossible to make out the exact nature of these duties; the following very brief intelligible passages will at least indicate their general direction:

> Enten caused the ewe to give birth to the lamb, the goat to give birth to the kid,
> Cow and calf he caused to multiply, much fat and milk he caused to be produced,
> In the plain, the heart of the *wild goat,* the sheep, and the donkey he made to rejoice,
> The birds of the heaven, in the wide earth he had them set up their nests,

The fish of the sea, in the swampland he had them lay their eggs,
In the palm-grove and vineyard he made to abound honey and
    wine,
The trees, wherever planted, he caused to bear fruit,
The furrows . . . ,
Grain and *crops* he caused to multiply,
Like Ashnan (the grain goddess), the kindly maid, he caused
    strength to appear.
Emesh brought into existence the trees and the fields, he made
    wide the stables and sheepfolds,
In the *farms* he multiplied the *produce*,
The . . . he caused to cover the earth,
The abundant harvest he caused to be brought into the houses,
    he caused the granaries to be heaped high.

But whatever the nature of their original duties, a violent quarrel breaks out between the two brothers. Several arguments ensue, and finally Emesh challenges Enten's claim to the position of "farmer of the gods." And so they betake themselves to Nippur where each states his case before Enlil. Thus Enten complains to Enlil:

PLATE XII. GODS OF VEGETATION

Three of the designs depict a deity in close relation with a plow. In the upper design two gods are guiding a plow, which is perhaps drawn by a lion and a worm-like dragon. In the second, a seated god is holding a plow in front of him. Behind him is a mountain from which sprouts a plant and on which an ibex is ascending; in front of him a deity leads a worshipper carrying a gazelle in his arms. In the lower design an unidentified deity holding a plow is travelling in a boat whose stern ends in a snake and whose prow ends in the body of a god who is propelling the boat.

The third design seems to depict an offering scene to the right of the inscription. A worshipper carrying a gazelle is followed by a goddess holding a vase, from which flow two streams of water. The worshipper stands before another goddess who may perhaps be identified as Inanna in the role of the goddess of war. But it is the two deities to the left of the inscriptions which interest us here mostly. Both seem to have ears of grain sprouting from their shoulders, but the male god is equipped with club and bow, while a ram frolics at his feet. He may perhaps be identified as Lahar, the cattle-god, while the goddess facing him may be Ashnan, the grain goddess (see p. 53).

(Reproduced, by permission of the Macmillan Company, from Henri Frankfort, *Cylinder Seals*, plates XX*a*, *d*, *e*, and *XIXe*.)

PLATE XII

GODS OF VEGETATION

(For description, see opposite page.)

> "O father Enlil, *knowledge* thou hast given me, I brought the
>   water of abundance,
> *Farm* I made touch *farm,* I heaped high the granaries,
> Like Ashnan, the kindly maid, I caused *strength* to appear;
> Now Emesh, the . . . , the *irreverent,* who knows not the heart
>   of the fields,
> *On my first strength, on my first power,* is encroaching;
> At the palace of the king . . ."

Emesh's version of the quarrel, which begins with several flattering phrases cunningly directed to win Enlil's
favor, is brief but as yet unintelligible.   Then:

> Enlil answers Emesh and Enten:
> "The life-producing water of all the lands, Enten is its *'knower,'*
> As farmer of the gods he has produced everything,
> Emesh, my son, how dost thou compare thyself with Enten, thy
>   brother?"

> The exalted word of Enlil whose meaning is profound,
> The decision taken, is unalterable, who dares transgress it!

> Emesh bent the knees before Enten,
> Into his house he brought . . . , the wine of the grape and the
>   date,
> Emesh presents Enten with gold, silver, and lapis lazuli,
> *In* brotherhood and friendship, *happily,* they pour out libations,
> Together *to act wisely and well they determined.*
> In the struggle between Emesh and Enten,
> Enten, the steadfast farmer of the gods, having proved greater
>   than Emesh,
> . . . O father Enlil, praise!

THE CREATION OF THE PICKAX

This poem consisting of 108 lines [52] is practically complete, although not a few of the passages still remain obscure and unintelligible.   It begins with a long introductory
passage which is of prime significance for the Sumerian
conception of the creation and organization of the universe.
If the following translation of this important passage seems
sodden, stilted, and obscure, the reader is asked to remem-
ber that although the meanings of most of the Sumerian
words and phrases are known, we still have little insight
into their overtones, into their connotations and implica-

tions. For the background and situation which these words and phrases imply and assume, still elude us; and it is this background and situation, part and parcel of the Sumerian mythological and religious pattern and well known to the Sumerian poet and his "reader," which are so vital to a full understanding of the text. It is only with the gradual accumulation of living contexts from Sumerian literature that we may hope to overcome this difficulty; as yet it is best to hew close to the literal word. The introductory passage reads:°

> The lord, that which is appropriate verily he caused to appear,
> The lord whose decisions are unalterable,
> Enlil, who brings up the seed of the land from the earth,
> *Took care* to move away heaven from earth,
> *Took care* to move away earth from heaven.
> *In order to make grow the creature which came forth,*
> In the "bond of heaven and earth" (Nippur) he stretched out the . . .

> He brought the pickax into existence, the "day" came forth,
> He *introduced labor,* decreed the fate,
> Upon the pickax and basket he directs the "power."
> Enlil made his pickax exalted,
> His pickax of gold, whose head is of lapis lazuli,
> The pickax of his house, of . . . silver and gold,
> His pickax whose . . . is of lapis lazuli,
> Whose *tooth* is a one-horned ox ascending a large wall.

> The lord called up the pickax, decrees its fate,
> He set the *kindu,* the holy crown, upon his head,
> The head of man he placed in the mould,
> Before Enlil *he* (man?) *covers* his land,
> Upon his black-headed people he looked steadfastly.
> The Anunnaki who stood about him,
> He placed *it* (the pickax?) as a gift in their hands,
> They soothe Enlil with prayer,
> They give the pickax to the black-headed people to hold.

After Enlil had created the pickax and decreed its exalted fate, the other important deities add to its powers and utility. The poem concludes with a long passage in which the usefulness of the pickax is described in glowing terms; the last lines read:

The pickax and the basket build cities,
The steadfast house the pickax builds, the steadfast house the
    pickax establishes,
The steadfast house it causes to prosper.

The house which rebels against the king,
The house which is not submissive to its king,
The pickax makes it submissive to the king.

Of the bad . . . plants it crushes the head,
Plucks at the roots, tears at the crown,
The pickax *spares* the . . . plants;
The pickax, its fate decreed by father Enlil,
The pickax is exalted.

CATTLE AND GRAIN

The myth [53] involving Lahar, the cattle-god, and his sister Ashnan, the grain-goddess, represents another variation of the Cain-Abel motif in Near East mythology. Lahar and Ashnan, according to our myth, were created in the creation chamber of the gods in order that the Anunnaki, the children and followers of the heaven-god An, might have food to eat and clothes to wear. But the Anunnaki were unable to make effective use of the products of these deities; it was to remedy this situation that man was created. All this is told in an introductory passage which, because of its significance for the Sumerian conception of the creation of man, is quoted in full on pages 72–73. The passage following the introduction is another poetic gem; it describes the descent of Lahar and Ashnan from heaven to earth and the cultural benefits which they bestow on mankind:

In those days Enki says to Enlil:
"Father Enlil, Lahar and Ashnan,
They who have been created in the Dulkug,
Let us cause them to descend from the Dulkug."

At the pure word of Enki and Enlil,
Lahar and Ashnan descended from the Dulkug.
For Lahar they (Enlil and Enki) set up the sheepfold,
Plants, herbs, and . . . they present to him;

For Ashnan they establish a house,
Plow and yoke they present to her.
Lahar standing in his sheepfold,
A shepherd increasing the bounty of the sheepfold is he;
Ashnan standing among the *crops,*
A maid kindly and bountiful is she.

Abundance of heaven . . . ,
Lahar and Ashnan caused to appear,
In the assembly they brought abundance,
In the land they brought the breath of life,
The decrees of the god they direct,
The contents of the warehouses they multiply,
The storehouses they fill full.

In the house of the poor, hugging the dust,
Entering they bring abundance;
The pair of them, wherever they stand,
Bring heavy increase into the house;
The place where they stand they sate, the place where they sit
    they supply,
They made good the heart of An and Enlil.

But then Lahar and Ashnan drank much wine and so
they began to quarrel in the *farms* and fields. In the arguments which ensued, each deity extolled its achievements and
belittled those of its opponent. Finally Enlil and Enki
intervened, but the end of the poem which contains their
decision is still wanting.

ENKI AND NINHURSAG: THE AFFAIRS OF THE WATER-GOD [p]

Both for intricacy of story and for simplicity of style,
this myth [57] is one of the most remarkable compositions in
our entire group. The hero is Enki, the great water-god of
the Sumerians, one of the four creating deities of Sumer;
his closest Greek counterpart is Poseidon. The place of our
story is Dilmun, a district which is perhaps to be identified
with eastern shores of the Persian Gulf and which in historical times, therefore, actually lay outside of Sumer
proper. Our poem begins with a description of Dilmun as
a land of innocence and bliss:

The land Dilmun is a pure place, the land Dilmun is a clean place,
The land Dilmun is a clean place, the land Dilmun is a bright place;
He who is all alone laid himself down in Dilmun,
The place, after Enki had laid himself by his wife,
That place is clean, that place is bright;
He who is all alone laid himself down in Dilmun,
The place, after Enki had laid himself by Ninsikil,
That place is clean, that place is bright.

In Dilmun the raven uttered no cries,
The *kite* uttered not the cry of the *kite*,
The lion killed not,
The wolf snatched not the lamb,
Unknown was the kid-killing dog,
Unknown was the grain-devouring *boar*,
The bird on high . . . not its *young*,
The dove . . . not the head,
The sick-eyed says not "I am sick-eyed,"
The sick-headed says not "I am sick-headed,"
Its (Dilmun's) old woman says not "I am an old woman,"
Its old man says not "I am an old man,"
Its unwashed maid is not . . . in the city,
He who *crosses* the river utters no . . . ,
The *overseer* does not . . . ,
The singer utters no wail,
By the side of the city he utters no lament.

What is wanting in this paradise land, however, is sweet water. And so the goddess of Dilmun, Ninsikil, pleads with Enki for fresh water. Enki heeds her plea and orders the sun-god Utu to bring forth fresh water from the earth for Dilmun. As a result:

Her city drinks the water of abundance,
Dilmun drinks the water of abundance,
Her wells of bitter water, behold they are become wells of good water,
Her fields and *farms* produced *crops* and grain,
Her city, behold it is become the house of the *banks and* quays of the land,
Dilmun, behold it is become the house of the *banks and* quays of the land.

Dilmun supplied with water, our poem next describes the birth of Uttu, the goddess of plants, a birth which results from the following rather intricate process. Enki first impregnates the goddess Ninhursag, or, to give her one of her other names, Nintu, the Sumerian goddess who in an earlier day may have been identical with Ki, the mother earth. Follows a period of gestation lasting nine days, the poet being careful to note that each day corresponds to a month in the human period of gestation; of this union is begotten the goddess Ninsar. This interesting passage runs as follows:

> Upon Ninhursag he *caused to flow* the "water of the heart,"
> She received the "water of the heart," the water of Enki.
> One day being her one month,
> Two days being her two months,
> Three days being her three months,
> Four days being her four months,
> Five days (being her five months,)
> Six days (being her six months,)
> Seven days (being her seven months,)
> Eight days (being her eight months,)
> Nine days being her nine months, the months of "womanhood,"
> Like . . . fat, like . . . fat, like good butter,
> Nintu, the mother of the land, like . . . fat, (like . . . fat, like good butter,)
> Gave birth to Ninsar.

Plate XIII. Enki and Ninhursag: the Affairs of the Water-god

This is a photograph of a tablet (4561 in the Nippur collection of the University Museum) published by Stephen Langdon more than 25 years ago under the title, "Sumerian Epic of Paradise, the Flood, and Fall of Man." [54] At the time of its publication, Sumerian grammatical and lexicographical studies had made relatively little scientific progress, and the contents of this difficult poem were largely misunderstood. The author's interpretation of the poem is largely the result of a more scientific approach to the linguistic problems, although the publication in 1930 by Henri de Genouillac of a duplicating fragment now in the Louvre [55] also proved of considerable help. The last 14 lines in the second column contain a passage which may be not inaptly entitled "The Birth of a Goddess"; for the translation and the transliteration, see page 56 and note 56.

PLATE XIII

ENKI AND NINHURSAG: THE AFFAIRS OF THE WATER-GOD

(For description, see opposite page.)

Ninsar in turn is impregnated by her father Enki and after nine days of gestation she gives birth to the goddess Ninkur. Ninkur, too, is then impregnated by Enki and so finally is born Uttu, the goddess of plants. To this plant-goddess now appears her great-grandmother Ninhursag, who offers her advice pertinent to her future relationship with Enki. Part of the passage is broken, and much of what is not broken I fail as yet to comprehend. But whatever the advice, Uttu follows it in all detail. As a result she is in turn impregnated by Enki and eight different plants sprout forth. But Enki eats up the plants; thus:

> Enki, in the swampland, in the swampland, lies stretched out,
> He says to his messenger Isimud:
> "What is this (plant), what is this (plant)?"
>
> His messenger, Isimud, answers him;
> "My king, this is the 'tree-plant'," he says to him.
> He cuts it off for him and he (Enki) eats it.
>
> *Enki:* "What is this, what is this?"
> *Isimud:* "My king, this is the 'honey-plant'."
> He tears it off for him and he eats it.

And so on until Enki has eaten all the eight plants. Thereupon Ninhursag, who, it will be recalled, is actually responsible for the creation of these plants, curses Enki.[58] The curse reads:

> "Until thou art dead, I shall not look upon thee with the 'eye of life'."

Having uttered the curse, Ninhursag disappears. The gods are chargrined; they "sit in the dust." Up speaks the fox to Enlil:

> "If I bring Ninhursag before thee, what shall be my reward?"

Enlil promises the fox a due reward and the latter succeeds in bringing her back; how he goes about this task is not clear, however, since part of the text is broken and much of the preserved part is as yet unintelligible. And so Ninhursag proceeds to remove the effects of her curse from the rapidly sinking Enki. This she achieves by giving birth to a special deity for each of Enki's pains. This passage which closes our poem runs as follows:

Ninhursag: "My brother, what hurts thee?"
Enki: "My . . . hurts me."
Ninhursag: "To the god Abu I gave birth for thee."

Ninhursag: "My brother, what hurts thee?"
Enki: "My *hip* hurts me."
Ninhursag: "To the god Nintul I gave birth for thee."

Ninhursag: "My brother, what hurts thee?"
Enki: "My tooth hurts me."
Ninhursag: "To the goddess Ninsutu I gave birth for thee."

Ninhursag: "My brother, what hurts thee?"
Enki: "My mouth hurts me."
Ninhursag: "To the goddess Ninkasi I gave birth for thee."

Ninhursag: "My brother, what hurts thee?"
Enki: "My . . . hurts me."
Ninhursag: "To the god Nazi I gave birth for thee."

Ninhursag: "My brother, what hurts thee?"
Enki: "My side hurts me."
Ninhursag: "To the goddess Dazimua I gave birth for thee."

Ninhursag: "My brother, what hurts thee?"
Enki: "My rib hurts me."
Ninhursag: "To the goddess Ninti I gave birth for thee."

Ninhursag: "My brother, what hurts thee?"
Enki: "My . . . hurts me."
Ninhursag: "To the god Enshagag I gave birth for thee."

Ninhursag: "*For* the little ones to which *I* gave birth . . ."
Enki: "Let Abu be the king of the plants,
　　Let Nintul be the lord of Magan,
　　Let Ninsutu marry Ninazu,
　　Let Ninkasi be (the goddess who) sates the heart,
　　Let Nazi marry Nindar,
　　Let Dazimua marry Ningishzida,
　　Let Ninti be the queen of the *month,*
　　Let Enshagag be the lord of Dilmun."

　　O Father Enki, praise!

And so, as the reader will note, the eight aches and pains which had come upon Enki as punishment for his eating the eight plants, were healed by the eight deities born of Ninhursag for that purpose. Moreover, the superficiality and barren artificiality of the concepts implied in this closing passage of our myth, although not apparent from the English translation, are brought out quite clearly by the Sumerian original. For the fact is that the actual relationship between each of the "healing" deities and the sickness which it is supposed to cure, is verbal and nominal only; this relationship manifests itself in the fact that the name of the deity contains in it part or all of the word signifying the corresponding aching part of Enki's body. In brief, it is only because the name of the deity *sounded* like the sick body-member that the makers of this myth were induced to associate the two; actually there is no organic relationship between them.

ENKI AND SUMER: THE ORGANIZATION OF THE EARTH AND ITS CULTURAL PROCESSES [q]

This composition [59] furnishes us with a detailed account of the activities of the water-god Enki, the Sumerian god of wisdom, in organizing the earth and establishing what might be termed law and order upon it. The first part of our poem, approximately one hundred lines, is too fragmentary for a reconstruction of its contents. When the poem becomes intelligible, Enki is decreeing the fate of Sumer:

> "O Sumer, great land, *of the lands* of the universe,
>> Filled with steadfast brightness, the people from sunrise to sunset obedient to the divine decrees,
>> Thy decrees are exalted decrees, unreachable,
>> Thy heart is profound, unfathomable,
>> Thy . . . is like heaven, untouchable.
>
> "The king, begotten, *adorns himself with lasting jewel,*
>> The lord, begotten, sets crown on head,
>> Thy lord is an honored lord; with An, the king, he sits in the shrine of heaven,
>> Thy king is the great mountain, the father Enlil,
>> Like . . . the father of all the lands.

"The Anunnaki, the great gods,
In thy midst have taken up their dwelling place,
In thy large *groves* they *consume* (their) food.

"O house of Sumer, may thy stables be many, may thy cows
    multiply,
May thy sheepfolds be many, may thy sheep be myriad,
May thy . . . stand,
May thy steadfast . . . lift hand to heaven,
May the Anunnaki decree the fates in thy midst."

Enki then goes to Ur, no doubt the capital of Sumer at
the time our poem was composed, and decrees its fate:

To Ur he came,
Enki, king of the abyss, decrees the fate:
"O city, well-supplied, washed by much water, firm standing ox,
Shrine of abundance of the land, knees opened, green like the
    'mountain,'
Hashur-forest, wide shade, . . . heroic,
Thy perfected decrees he has directed,
The great mountain, Enlil, in the universe has uttered thy
    exalted name;
O thou city whose fates have been decreed by Enki,
O thou shrine Ur, neck to heaven mayest thou rise."

Enki then comes to Meluhha, the "black mountain,"
perhaps to be identified with the eastern coast of Africa.
Remarkably enough, Enki is almost as favorably disposed

PLATE XIV. ENKI, THE WATER-GOD

In the latter half of the third millennium the water-god Enki played a pre-
dominant role in Sumerian religion and myth. This plate gives a graphic picture
of his activities. The upper design depicts Enki with flowing streams, swimming
fishes, and what may be sprouting plants, travelling in a boat along the Eridu
marshland. In the second design four deities are approaching the seated Enki;
the second carries a plow. The third design depicts Enki sitting in judgment.
His messenger, the two-faced Isimud, is followed by a deity carrying a plant; the
latter is followed by another deity who carries slung over his shoulder a mace to
which the accused bird-man is tied by the feet. The lower design depicts another
version of the same scene. Before Enki, seated in judgment, Isimud leads the
accused bird-man, who is followed by another deity and a worshipper.

(Reproduced, by permission of the Macmillan Company, from Henri Frankfort, *Cylinder Seals*, plates XX*f*, XXI*e*, and XXXIII*d, f*.)

PLATE XIV

ENKI, THE WATER-GOD

(For description, see opposite page.)

to this land as to Sumer itself. He blesses its trees and reeds, its oxen and birds, its silver and gold, its bronze and copper, its human beings. From Meluhha, Enki goes to the Tigris and Euphrates Rivers. He fills them with sparkling water and appoints the god Enbilulu, the *"knower"* of rivers, in charge. Enki then fills the rivers with fishes and makes a deity described as the "son of Kesh" responsible for them. He next turns to the sea (Persian Gulf), sets up its rules, and appoints the goddess Sirara in charge.

Enki now calls to the winds and appoints over them the god Ishkur, who has charge of the "silver lock of the 'heart' of heaven." The plow and yoke, fields and vegetation, are next on the list:

> The plow and the yoke he directed,
> The great prince Enki caused the . . . ox to . . .;
> To the pure *crops* he *roared*,
> In the steadfast field he made grain grow;
> The lord, the jewel and ornament of the plain,
> The . . . farmer of Enlil,
> Enkimdu, him of the canals and ditches,
> Enki placed in their charge.

> The lord called to the steadfast field, he caused it to produce much grain,
> Enki made it bring forth its small and large beans . . . ,
> The . . . grains he heaped up for the granary,
> Enki added granary to granary,
> With Enlil he increases abundance in the land;
> Her whose head is . . . , whose face is . . . ,
> The lady who . . . , the might of the land, the steadfast *support* of the black-headed people,
> Ashnan, strength of all things,
> Enki placed in charge.

Enki now turns to the pickax and the brickmold, and appoints the brick-god Kabta in charge. He then directs the building implement *gugun,* lays foundations and builds houses, and places them under the charge of Mushdamma, the "great builder of Enlil." He then fills the plain with plant and animal life and places Sumugan, "king of the 'mountain'," in control. Finally Enki builds stables and sheepfolds, fills them with milk and fat, and puts them in the care of the sheperd-god Dumuzi. The rest of our text is destroyed and we do not know how the poem ends.

ENKI AND ERIDU: THE JOURNEY OF THE WATER-GOD TO NIPPUR

One of the oldest and most venerated cities in Sumer was Eridu, which lies buried to-day under the mound Abu-Shahrain; a thorough excavation of this significant site would in all probability immensely enrich our knowledge of Sumerian culture and civilization, especially in their more spiritual aspects. According to one Sumerian tradition, it was the oldest city in Sumer, the first of the five cities founded before the flood; our myth, on the other hand, implies that the city Nippur preceded it in age. In this city, which in ancient times must have been situated on the Persian Gulf, the water-god Enki, also known as Nudimmud, builds his "sea-house": [60]

> After the water of *creation* had been decreed,
> After the name *hegal* (abundance), born in heaven,
> Like plant and herb had clothed the land,
> The lord of the abyss, the king Enki,
> Enki, the lord who decrees the fates,
> Built his house of silver and lapis lazuli;
> Its silver and lapis lazuli, *like sparkling light,*
> The father *fashioned fittingly* in the abyss.

> The (*creatures of*) *bright countenance* and wise, coming forth
>   from the abyss,
> Stood all about the lord Nudimmud;
> The pure house he built, he adorned it with lapis lazuli,
> He ornamented it greatly with gold,
> In Eridu he built the house of the *water-bank,*
> Its brickwork, word-uttering, advice-giving,
> Its . . . like an ox roaring,
> The house of Enki, the *oracles* uttering.

Follows a long passage in which Isimud, the messenger of Enki, sings the praises of the "sea-house." Then Enki *raises* the city Eridu *from the abyss* and makes it *float* over the water like a lofty mountain. Its green fruit-bearing gardens he fills with birds; fishes, too, he makes abundant. Enki is now ready to proceed by boat to Nippur to obtain Enlil's blessing for his newly-built city and temple. He therefore rises from the abyss:

> When Enki rises, the fish . . . rise,
> The abyss stands in wonder,
> In the sea joy enters,
> Fear comes over the deep,
> Terror holds the exalted river,
> The Euphrates, the South Wind *lifts it in waves*.

And so Enki seats himself in his boat and first arrives in Eridu itself; here he slaughters many oxen and sheep. He then proceeds to Nippur where immediately upon his arrival he prepares all kinds of drinks for the gods and especially for Enlil. Then:

> Enki in the shrine Nippur,
> Gives his father Enlil bread to eat,
> In the first place he seated An (the heaven-god),
> Next to An he seated Enlil,
> Nintu he seated at the "big side,"
> The Anunnaki seated themselves one after the other.

And so the gods feast and banquet until their hearts become "good" and Enlil is ready to pronounce his blessing:

> Enlil says to the Anunnaki:
> "Ye great gods who are standing about,
> My son has built a house, the king Enki;
> Eridu, like a mountain, he has raised up from the earth,
> In a good place he has built it.
>
> Eridu, the clean place, where none may enter,
> The house built of silver, adorned with lapis lazuli,
> The house directed by the seven *"lyre-songs,"* given over to incantation,
> *With pure songs . . . ,*
> The abyss, the shrine of the goodness of Enki, befitting the divine decrees,
> Eridu, the pure house having been built,
> O Enki, praise!"

INANNA AND ENKI: THE TRANSFER OF THE ARTS OF
CIVILIZATION FROM ERIDU TO ERECH

This magnificent myth with its particularly charming story involves Inanna, the queen of heaven, and Enki, the lord of wisdom. Its contents are of profound significance for the study of the history and progress of civilization, since it contains a list of over one hundred divine decrees governing all those cultural achievements which, according to the more or less superficial analysis of the Sumerian scribes and thinkers, made up the warp and woof of Sumerian civilization. As early as 1911 a fragment belonging to this myth and located in the University Museum at Philadelphia was published by David W. Myhrman.[62] Three years later, Arno Poebel published another Philadelphia tablet inscribed with part of the composition;[61] this is a large, well-preserved six-column tablet whose upper left

---

PLATES XV AND XVI. INANNA AND ENKI: THE TRANSFER OF THE ARTS OF CIVILIZATION FROM ERIDU TO ERECH

Plate XV is the obverse of a large six-column tablet (15283 in the Nippur collection of the University Museum) published by Poebel in 1914;[61] its upper left corner is broken away. Plate XVI illustrates three fragments belonging to the same poem. The large fragment (13571 in the Nippur collection of the University Museum) was published by Myhrman in 1911.[62] Below the large fragment, on the left, are the obverse and reverse of a small fragment (4151 in the Nippur collection of the Museum of the Ancient Orient) copied by the author in Istanbul and hitherto unpublished. *In all probability it is the very corner piece broken away from the Philadelphia tablet illustrated on plate XV.* To the right are the obverse and reverse of another small fragment (2724 in the Nippur collection of the Museum of the Ancient Orient) copied by the author in Istanbul and hitherto unpublished. Small as it is, this piece proved instrumental in supplying the motivating link to the story. For the translation and the transliteration of the first eight lines of the passage in which Enki presents the arts of civilization to the goddess Inanna, see page 66 and note 65.

Another significant verse in this passage reads:[66]

"O name of my power, O name of my power,
　To the bright Inanna, my daughter, I shall present . . .
　The arts of woodworking, metalworking, writing, toolmaking, leather-
　　　working, . . . building, basketweaving."
Pure Inanna took them.

PLATE XV

INANNA AND ENKI: THE TRANSFER OF THE ARTS OF CIVILIZATION
FROM ERIDU TO ERECH

(For description, see opposite page.)

PLATE XVI

INANNA AND ENKI: THE TRANSFER OF THE ARTS OF CIVILIZATION
FROM ERIDU TO ERECH

(For description, see page 64.)

corner was broken off. This broken corner piece I was fortunate enough to discover in 1937, twenty-three years later,
in the Museum of the Ancient Orient at Istanbul.[63] As
early as 1914, therefore, a large part of the myth had been
copied and published. However, no translation was attempted in all these years since the story seemed to make
no connected sense; and what could be made out, seemed to
lack intelligent motivation. In 1937 I located and copied
in Istanbul a small piece [64] which supplied the missing clue,
and as a result, this tale of the all too human Sumerian gods
can now be told.[67]

Inanna, queen of heaven, and tutelary goddess of Erech,
is anxious to increase the welfare and prosperity of her
city, to make it the center of Sumerian civilization, and thus
to exalt her own name and fame. She therefore decides to
go to Eridu, the ancient and hoary seat of Sumerian culture where Enki, the Lord of Wisdom, who "knows the very
heart of the gods," dwells in his watery abyss, the Abzu.
For Enki has under his charge all the divine decrees that
are fundamental to civilization. And if she can obtain
them, by fair means or foul, and bring them to her beloved
city Erech, its glory and her own will indeed be unsur-
passed. As she approaches the Abzu of Eridu, Enki, no
doubt taken in by her charms, calls his messenger Isimud
and thus addresses him:

> "Come, my messenger, Isimud, give ear to my instructions,
> A word I will say to thee, take my word.
> The maid, all alone, has directed her step to the Abzu,
> Inanna, all alone, has directed her step to the Abzu,
> Have the maid enter the Abzu of Eridu,
> Have Inanna enter the Abzu of Eridu,
> Give her to eat barley cake with butter,
> Pour for her cold water that freshens the heart,
> Give her to drink date-wine in the 'face of the lion,'
> . . . for her . . . , make for her . . . ,
> At the pure table, the table of heaven,
> Speak to Inanna words of greeting."

Isimud does exactly as bidden by his master, and Inanna
and Enki sit down to feast and banquet. After their hearts
had become happy with drink, Enki exclaims:

"O name of my power, O name of my power,
To the pure Inanna, my daughter, I shall present . . . ,
Lordship, . . .-ship, godship, the tiara exalted and enduring,
the throne of kingship."

Pure Inanna took them.

"O name of my power, O name of my power,
To the pure Inanna, my daughter, I shall present . . . ,
The exalted scepter, *staffs,* the exalted shrine, sheperdship,
kingship."

Pure Inanna took them.

He thus presents, several at a time, over one hundred divine decrees which are the basis of the culture pattern of Sumerian civilization. And when it is realized that this myth was inscribed as early as 2000 B. C. and that the concepts involved were no doubt current centuries earlier, it is no exaggeration to state that no other civilization, outside of the Egyptian, can at all compare in age and quality with that developed by the Sumerians. Among these divine decrees presented by Enki to Inanna are those referring to lordship, godship, the exalted and enduring crown, the throne of kingship, the exalted scepter, the exalted shrine, sheperdship, kingship, the numerous priestly offices, truth, descent into the nether world and ascent from it, the "standard," the flood, sexual intercourse and prostitution, the *legal* tongue and the *libellous* tongue, art, the holy cult chambers, the "hierodule of heaven," music, eldership, heroship and power, enmity, straightforwardness, the destruction of cities and lamentation, rejoicing of the heart, falsehood, the rebel land, goodness and justice, the craft of the carpenter, metal worker, scribe, smith, leather worker, mason, and basket weaver, wisdom and understanding, purification, fear and *outcry,* the kindling flame and the *consuming* flame, weariness, the shout of victory, counsel, the troubled heart, judgment and decision, exuberance, musical instruments.

Inanna is only too happy to accept the gifts offered her by the drunken Enki. She takes them, loads them on her "boat of heaven," and makes off for Erech with her precious cargo. But after the effects of the banquet had worn off, Enki noticed that the divine decrees were gone from their usual place. He turns to Isimud and the latter informs him that he, Enki himself, had presented them to his daughter Inanna. The upset Enki greatly rues his munificence and decides to prevent the "boat of heaven" from reaching Erech at all costs. He therefore dispatches his messenger Isimud together with a group of sea monsters to follow Inanna and her boat to the first of the seven stopping stations that are situated between the Abzu of Eridu and Erech. Here the sea monsters are to seize the "boat of heaven" from Inanna; Inanna, herself, however, must be permitted to continue her journey to Erech afoot. The passage covering Enki's instructions to Isimud and Isimud's conversation with Inanna, who reproaches her father Enki as an "Indian-giver," will undoubtedly go down as a classic poetic gem. It runs as follows:

> The prince calls his messenger Isimud,
> Enki gives the word to the "good name of heaven":
> "Oh my messenger Isimud, 'my good name of heaven'."

> "Oh my king Enki, here I stand, *forever* is praise."

> "The 'boat of heaven,' where now has it arrived?"

> "At the *quay* Idal it has arrived."

> "Go, and let the *sea monsters* seize it from her."

Isimud does as bidden, overtakes the "boat of heaven," and says to Inanna:

> "Oh my queen, thy father has sent me to thee,
> Oh Inanna, thy father has sent me to thee,
> Thy father, exalted is his speech,
> Enki, exalted is his utterance,
> His great words are not *to go unheeded*."

> Holy Inanna answers him:
> "My father, what has he spoken to thee, what has he said to thee?
> His great words that are not *to go unheeded*, what pray are they?"

> "My king has spoken to me,
> Enki has said to me:
> 'Let Inanna go to Erech,
> But thou, bring me back the "boat of heaven" to Eridu'."

Holy Inanna says to the messenger Isimud:
"My father, why pray has he changed his word to me,
Why has he broken his righteous word to me,
Why has he defiled his great words to me?
My father has spoken to me falsehood, has spoken to me false-
    hood,
Falsely has he uttered the name of his power, the name of the
    Abzu."

Barely had she uttered these words,
The *sea monsters* seized the "boat of heaven."
Inanna says to her messenger Ninshubur:
"Come, my true messenger of Eanna,
My messenger of favorable words,
My carrier of true words,
Whose hand never falters, whose foot never falters,
Save the 'boat of heaven,' and Inanna's presented decrees."

This Ninshubur does. But Enki is persistent. He
sends Isimud accompanied by various sea monsters to seize
the "boat of heaven" at each of the seven stopping points
between Eridu and Erech. And each time Ninshubur
comes to Inanna's rescue. Finally Inanna and her boat
arrive safe and sound at Erech, where amidst jubilation
and feasting on the part of its delighted inhabitants, she
unloads the divine decrees one at a time. The poem ends
with a speech addressed by Enki to Inanna, but the text is
seriously damaged and it is not clear whether it is recon-
ciliatory or retaliatory in character.

THE CREATION OF MAN [8]

The composition narrating the creation of man has been
found inscribed on two duplicating tablets: one is a Nippur
tablet in our University Museum; the other is in the Louvre,
which acquired it from an antique dealer. In spite of the
fact that by 1934 the Louvre tablet and the greater part
of the University Museum tablet had already been copied
and published,[72] the contents remained unintelligible. Primarily responsible for this unfortunate situation is the fact
that our University Museum tablet, which is better preserved than the Louvre fragment, arrived in Philadelphia

some four or five decades ago, broken into four parts. By 1919 two of the pieces had already been recognized and joined; these were copied and published by Stephen Langdon.[68] In 1934 Edward Chiera published the third piece [69] but failed to recognize that it joined the two pieces published by Langdon in 1919. It was the discovery of this fact, together with the identifying of the fourth and still unpublished piece [70] which *joins* the three published pieces, that enabled me to arrange the contents in the proper order. It should be emphasized here that the approximately one hundred and fifty lines which make up the text of our poem still present numerous crucial breaks; many of the lines are poorly preserved.[73] Moreover, the linguistic difficulties in this composition are particularly burdensome; not a few of the crucial words are met here for the first time in Sumerian literature. The translation is therefore full of gaps and its tentative character must be underlined. Nevertheless it does present the fullest picture thus far available of the concepts concerned with the creation of man as current in Sumer during the third millennium B. C.

Among the oldest known conceptions of the creation of man are those of the Hebrews and the Babylonians; the former is narrated in the book of Genesis, the latter forms part of the Babylonian "Epic of Creation." According to the Biblical story, or at least according to one of its versions, man was fashioned from clay for the purpose of ruling over all the animals. In the Babylonian myth, man was made of the blood of one of the more troublesome of the gods who was killed for that purpose; he was created primarily in order to serve the gods and free them from the need of working for their bread. According to our Sumerian poem, which antedates both the Hebrew and the Babylonian versions by more than a millennium, man was fashioned of clay as in the Biblical version. The purpose for which he was created, however, was to free the gods from laboring for their sustenance, as in the Babylonian version.

The poem begins with what may be a description of the difficulties of the gods in procuring their bread, especially, as might have been expected, after the female deities had come into being. The gods complain, but Enki, the water-god, who, as the Sumerian god of wisdom, might have been expected to come to their aid, is lying asleep in the deep and fails to hear them. Thereupon his mother, the primeval sea, "the mother who gave birth to all the gods," brings the tears of the gods before Enki, saying:

> "O my son, rise from thy bed, from thy . . . work what is wise,
> Fashion *servants* of the gods, may they produce their . . ."

Enki gives the matter thought, leads forth the host of "good and princely *fashioners*" and says to his mother, Nammu, the primeval sea:

> O my mother, the *creature* whose name thou hast uttered, it exists,
>> Bind upon it the . . . of the gods;
> *Mix* the heart of the clay that is over the abyss,
> The good and princely *fashioners* will *thicken* the clay,
>> Thou, do thou bring the *limbs* into existence;
> Ninmah (the earth-mother goddess) will work above thee,
> . . . (goddesses of birth) will stand by thee at thy fashioning;
> O my mother, decree thou its (the new-born's) fate,
>> Ninmah will bind upon it the . . . of the gods,
> . . . as man . . .

After a break of several lines, whose contents, if ever recovered, should prove most illuminating, the poem de-

---

PLATES XVII AND XVIII. THE CREATION OF MAN

These plates illustrate the obverse of the very same tablet. On plate XVII the tablet is still in *three* separate pieces (13386, 11327, and 2168, before "joining," in the Nippur collection of the University Museum). Actually the tablet arrived in Philadelphia in *four* separate pieces. The lower piece on plate XVII is itself composed of two fragments which had already been joined in the University Museum sometime before 1919, when it was published by Langdon.[68] The large upper fragment was published by Chiera in 1934.[69] The fourth piece [70] has hitherto remained unpublished. Plate XVIII shows the same tablet with all the pieces joined. The lower part of the first column contains the first part of the passage in which Enki, the water-god, instructs his mother Nammu, the goddess who begot heaven and earth and all the gods, how to fashion man. For the translation and the transliteration, see page 70 and note 71.

PLATE XVII

THE CREATION OF MAN

(For description, see opposite page.)

PLATE XVIII

THE CREATION OF MAN

(For description, see page 70.)

scribes a feast arranged by Enki for the gods, no doubt to commemorate man's creation.   At this feast Enki and Ninmah drink much wine and become somewhat exuberant. Thereupon Ninmah takes some of the clay which is over the abyss and fashions six different types of individuals, while Enki decrees their fate and gives them bread to eat.   The character of only the last two types is intelligible; these are the barren woman and the sexless or eunuch type.   The lines read:

> The . . . she (Ninmah) made into a woman who cannot give birth.
> Enki upon seeing the woman who cannot give birth,
> Decreed her fate, destined her to be stationed in the "woman house."
>
> The . . . she (Ninmah) made into one who has no male organ, who has no female organ.
> Enki, upon seeing him who has no male organ, who has no female organ,
> To stand before the king, decreed as his fate.

After Ninmah had created these six types of man, Enki decides to do some creating of his own.   The manner in which he goes about it is not clear, but whatever it is that he does, the resulting creature is a failure; it is weak and feeble in body and spirit.   Enki is now anxious that Ninmah help this forlorn creature; he therefore addresses her as follows:

> "Of him whom thy hand has fashioned, I have decreed the fate,
> Have given him bread to eat;
> Do thou decree the fate of him whom my hand has fashioned,
> Do thou give him bread to eat."

Ninmah tries to be good to the creature but to no avail. She talks to him but he fails to answer.   She gives him bread to eat but he does not reach out for it.   He can neither sit nor stand, nor bend the knees.   A long conversation between Enki and Ninmah then follows, but the tablets are so badly broken at this point that it is impossible to make out the sense of the contents.   Finally Ninmah seems to utter a curse against Enki because of the sick, lifeless creature which he produced, a curse which Enki seems to accept as his due.

In addition to the creation poem outlined above, a detailed description of the purpose for which mankind was created is given in the introduction to the myth "Cattle and Grain" (see p. 53); it runs as follows. After the Anunnaki, the heaven-gods, had been born, but before the creation of Lahar, the cattle-god, and Ashnan, the grain-goddess, there existed neither cattle nor grain. The gods therefore "knew not" the eating of bread nor the dressing of garments. The cattle-god Lahar and the grain-goddess Ashnan were then created in the creation chamber of heaven, but still the gods remained unsated. It was then that man "was given breath," for the sake of the welfare of the sheepfolds and "good things" of the gods. This introduction reads as follows:

> After on the mountain of heaven and earth,
> An (the heaven-god) had caused the Anunnaki (his followers) to be born,
> Because the name Ashnan (the grain-goddess) had not been born, had not been fashioned,
> Because Uttu (the goddess of plants) had not been fashioned,
> Because to Uttu no temenos had been set up,
> There was no ewe, no lamb was dropped,
> There was no goat, no kid was dropped,
> The ewe did not give birth to its two lambs,
> The goat did not give birth to its three kids.
>
> Because the name of Ashnan, the wise, and Lahar (the cattle-god),
> The Anunnaki, the great gods, did not know,
> The . . . grain of thirty days did not exist,
> The . . . grain of forty days did not exist,
> The small grains, the grain of the mountain, the grain of the pure living creatures did not exist.
>
> Because Uttu had not been born, because the crown (of vegetation?) had not been raised,
> Because the lord . . . had not been born,
> Because Sumugan, the god of the plain, had not come forth,
> Like mankind when first created,

They (the Anunnaki) knew not the eating of bread,
Knew not the dressing of garments,
Ate plants with their mouth like sheep,
Drank water from the ditch.

In those days, in the creation chamber of the gods,
In their house Dulkug, Lahar and Ashnan were fashioned;
The produce of Lahar and Ashnan,
The Anunnaki of the Dulkug eat, but remain unsated;
In their pure sheepfolds milk, . . . , and good things,
The Anunnaki of the Dulkug drink, but remain unsated;
For the sake of the good things in their pure sheepfolds,
Man was given breath.

The creation of man concludes our study of Sumerian cosmogony, of the theories and concepts evolved by the Sumerians to explain the origin of the universe and the existence of gods and men. It cannot be sufficiently stressed that the Sumerian cosmogonic concepts, early as they are, are by no means *primitive.* They reflect the mature thought and reason of the thinking Sumerian as he contemplated the forces of nature and the character of his own existence. When these concepts are analyzed; when the theological cloak and polytheistic trappings are removed (*although this is by no means always possible at present because of the limited character of our material as well as of our understanding and interpretation of its contents*), the Sumerian creation concepts indicate a keenly observing mentality as well as an ability to draw and formulate pertinent conclusions from the data observed. Thus *rationally* expressed, the Sumerian comogonic concepts may be summarized as follows:

1. First was the primeval *sea;* it is not unlikely that it was conceived by the Sumerian as *eternal* and *uncreated.*

2. The primeval sea engendered a *united heaven and earth.*

3. Heaven and earth were conceived as *solid* elements. Between them, however, and *from them,* came the gaseous element *air,* whose main characteristic is that of expansion. Heaven and earth were thus separated by the expanding element *air.*

4. Air, being lighter and far less dense than either heaven or earth, succeeded in producing the *moon,* which may have been conceived by the Sumerians as made of the same stuff as air. The *sun* was conceived as born of the *moon;* that is, it emanated and developed from the moon just as the latter emanated and developed from air.

5. After heaven and earth had been separated, *plant, animal,* and *human* life became possible on earth; all life seems to have been conceived as resulting from a union of air, earth, and water; the sun, too, was probably involved. Unfortunately in this matter of production and reproduction of plant and animal life on earth, our extant material is very difficult to penetrate.

Transferred into theological language, these rationalistic Sumerian concepts may be described as follows:

1. First was the goddess *Nammu,* the primeval sea personified.

2. The goddess *Nammu* gave birth to *An,* the male heaven-god, and *Ki,* the earth-goddess.

3. The union of *An* and *Ki* produced the air-god *Enlil,* who proceeded to separate the heaven-father *An* from the earth-mother *Ki.*

4. *Enlil,* the air-god, now found himself living in utter darkness, with the sky, which may have been conceived by the Sumerians as made of pitch-dark lapis lazuli, forming the ceiling and walls of his house, and the surface of the earth, its floor. He therefore begot the moon-god *Nanna* to brighten the darkness of his house. The moon-god *Nanna* in turn begot the sun-god *Utu,* who became brighter than his father. It is not without interest to note here that the idea that the son, the begotten one, becomes stronger than the father, the begetter—in a deeper sense this is actually what happens in the development which we term *progress*—is native to the philosophy and psychology of the Near East. *Enlil,* the air-god, for example, becomes in historical times more powerful than his father *An,* the heaven-god. At a later date *Marduk,* the god of the Semitic Babylonians, becomes more powerful than his father *Enki,*

the water-god. In the Christian dogma, Christ, the son, becomes in many ways more significant and pertinent for man and his salvation than God, the father.

5. *Enlil,* the air-god, now unites with his mother *Ki,* the earth-goddess. It is from this union but with considerable help from *Enki,* the water-god, that the vegetable and animal life is produced on earth. Man, on the other hand, seems to be the product of the combined efforts of the goddess *Nammu,* the primeval sea; of the goddess *Ninmah,* who may perhaps be identified with *Ki,* the mother earth; and finally of the water-god *Enki.* Just what is involved in this particular combination—and there is every reason to believe that in view of the more or less superficial data of the times there was good logic behind it and not mere playful fantasy—it is difficult to gather from our present material and limited understanding.

CHAPTER III

MYTHS OF KUR

One of the most difficult groups of concepts to identify and interpret is that represented by the Sumerian word *kur*. That one of its primary meanings is "mountain" is attested by the fact that the sign used for it is actually a pictograph representing a mountain. From the meaning "mountain" developed that of "foreign land," since the mountainous countries bordering Sumer were a constant menace to its people. *Kur* also came to mean "land" in general; Sumer itself is described as *kur-gal,* "great land."

But in addition the Sumerian word *kur* represented a cosmic concept. Thus it seems to be identical to a certain extent with the Sumerian *ki-gal,* "great below." Like *ki-gal,* therefore, it has the meaning "nether world"; indeed in such poems as "Inanna's Descent to the Nether World" and "Gilgamesh, Enkidu, and the Nether World," the word regularly used for "nether world" is *kur*. *Kur* thus cosmically conceived is the empty space between the earth's crust and the primeval sea. Moreover, it is not improbable that the monstrous creature that lived at the bottom of the "great below" immediately over the primeval waters is also called Kur; if so, this monster Kur would correspond to a certain extent to the Babylonian Tiamat. In three of our "Myths of Kur," it is one or the other of these cosmic aspects of the word *kur* which is involved.

THE DESTRUCTION OF KUR: THE SLAYING OF THE DRAGON

It is now more than half a century since the Babylonian "Epic of Creation," which centers largely about the slaying of the goddess Tiamat and her host of dragons, has been available to scholar and layman. Inscribed in Accadian, a Semitic language, on tablets dating from the first millennium B. C.—tablets that are therefore later by more than a

millennium than our Sumerian literary inscriptions—it is
quoted and cited in the major works concerned with mythology and religion as an example of Semitic myth-making.
But even a surface examination of its contents clearly reveals Sumerian origin and influence. The very names of its
protagonists are in large part Sumerian. What prevented
scholars from making any effective comparisons, is the fact
that so little was known of any original Sumerian tales involving the slaying of a dragon. It is therefore deeply
gratifying to be in a position to present the contents of what
are probably three distinct Sumerian versions of the dragon-
slaying myth. Two of these are almost entirely unknown;
their contents have been reconstructed and deciphered by
me in the course of the past several years. The third has
been known to a certain extent for a number of decades, but
the new material in Istanbul and Philadelphia adds considerably to its contents and clarity.

Obviously enough the dragon-slaying motif is not con-
fined to the myths of Mesopotamia. Almost all peoples and
all ages have had their dragon stories. In Greece, especially, these tales, involving both gods and heroes, were
legion. There was hardly a Greek hero who did not slay
his dragon, although Heracles and Perseus are perhaps the
best known dragon-killers. With the rise of Christianity,
the heroic feat was transferred to the saints; witness the
story of "St. George and the Dragon" and its numerous
and ubiquitous parallels. The names are different and the
details vary from story to story and from place to place.
But that at least some of the incidents go back to a more
original and central source, is more than likely. And since
the dragon-slaying theme was an important motif in the
Sumerian mythology of the third millennium B. C., it is
not unreasonable to assume that many a thread in the tex-
ture of the Greek and early Christian dragon tales winds
back to Sumerian sources.

As stated above, we may have three versions of the
slaying-of-the-dragon myth as current in Sumer in the third
millennium B. C. The first involves the Sumerian water-

3—myths

1

god Enki, whose closest parallel among the Greek gods is Poseidon. The hero of the second is Ninurta, prototype of the Babylonian god Marduk when playing the role of the "hero of the gods" in the Babylonian "Epic of Creation." In the third it is Inanna, counterpart of the Semitic Ishtar, who plays the leading role. In all three versions, however, the monster to be destroyed is termed Kur. Its exact form and shape are still uncertain, but there are indications that in the first two versions it is conceived as a large serpent which lived in the bottom of the "great below" where the latter came in contact with the primeval waters. For at least according to one of the versions, when Kur is destroyed, these waters rise to the surface of the earth and all cultivation with its resulting vegetation becomes impossible.

It is the first of the three versions of the slaying of the dragon which seems to be the more original; the details of the story, few as they are, are significant and instructive. For in the first place, the battle between the god and Kur seems to take place not long after the separation of heaven and earth. Moreover, the crime involved is probably that of abducting a goddess; it therefore brings to mind the Greek story of the rape of Persephone. Finally, it is the water-god Enki, the "god of wisdom," one of the ruling and creating deities of Sumer, who is the hero of the story. Un-

---

PLATE XIX. GODS AND DRAGONS

The first and second designs depict the combat of a god with a snakelike dragon. It is to be noted, however, that both designs are on cylinder seals of the first millennium B. C., and it is doubtful whether they depict the Ninurta-Kur battle of our Sumerian myth. The third design shows a fire-spitting winged dragon drawing the chariot of a god who had probably subjugated it in battle; between the two wings stands a nude female deity. Closely related to this scene is that of the fourth design, where the god and goddess are each riding on the back of a winged dragon.

(The first and second designs are from A. Jeremias, *Handbuch der altorientalischen Geisteskultur* (Berlin and Leipzig, 1929), page 431. The third and fourth designs are reproduced, by permission of the Macmillan Company, from Henri Frankfort, *Cylinder Seals*, plate XXIIa, d.)

PLATE XIX

GODS AND DRAGONS

(For description, see opposite page.)

fortunately we have only a very brief laconic passage from which to reconstruct our story; the tablets on which the details of the myth are inscribed are still lying no doubt in the ruins of Sumer. What we do have is part of the introductory prologue to the epic tale "Gilgamesh, Enkidu, and the Nether World," whose contents have been described on page 30 ff. Briefly sketched, this version of our story runs as follows:

After heaven and earth had been separated, An, the heaven-god, carried off the heaven, while Enlil, the air-god, carried off the earth. It was then that the foul deed was committed. The goddess Ereshkigal was carried off violently into the nether world, perhaps by Kur itself. Thereupon Enki, the water-god, whose Sumerian origin is uncertain, but who toward the end of the third millennium B. C. gradually became one of the most important deities of the Sumerian pantheon, set out in a boat, in all probability to attack Kur and avenge the abduction of the goddess Ereshkigal. Kur fought back savagely with all kinds of stones, large and small. Moreover it attacked Enki's boat, front and rear, with the primeval waters which it no doubt controlled. Here our brief prologue passage ends, since the author of "Gilgamesh, Enkidu, and the Nether World" is not interested in the dragon story primarily but is anxious to proceed with the Gilgamesh tale. And so we are left in the dark as to the outcome of the battle. There is little doubt, however, that Enki was victorious. Indeed it is not at all unlikely that the myth was evolved in large part for the purpose of explaining why, in historical times, Enki, like the Greek Poseidon, was conceived as a sea-god; why he is described as "lord of the abyss"; and why his temple in Eridu was designated as the "sea-house." [74]

The second version of the slaying-of-the-dragon myth is particularly significant since this is the version which must have been utilized in large part by the Semitic redactors of the Babylonian "Epic of Creation." [74] The story is part of a large epic tale of over six hundred lines, best entitled

"The Feats and Exploits of Ninurta." The contents can now be reconstructed in large part from at least 49 tablets and fragments, 30 of which have been copied and published by various scholars in the course of the past several decades; a large part of the text has therefore been known for some time.[75] Nevertheless, because of the numerous breaks and gaps, several of the more important pieces could not be properly arranged. This situation was eased to a considerable extent when I located in Istanbul and Philadelphia more than a score of additional pieces belonging to the poem.[t] And so, while the text is still badly broken at numerous crucial points, the contents as a whole can now be reconstructed with a fair degree of certainty.[76]

Hero of the tale is Ninurta, the warrior-god, who was conceived by the Sumerians as the son of Enlil, the air-god. After a hymnal introduction the story begins with an address to Ninurta by Sharur, his personified weapon. For some reason not stated in the text as yet available, Sharur has set its mind against Kur. In its speech, therefore, which is full of phrases extolling the heroic qualities and deeds of Ninurta, it urges Ninurta to attack and destroy Kur. Ninurta sets out to do as bidden. At first, however, he seems to have met more than his match and he "flees like a bird." Once again, however, Sharur addresses him with reassuring and encouraging words. Ninurta now attacks Kur fiercely with all the weapons at his command, and Kur is completely destroyed.

With the destruction of Kur, however, a serious calamity overtakes the land. The primeval waters which Kur had held in check rise to the surface and as a result of their violence no fresh water can reach the fields and gardens. The gods of the land who "carried the pickax and the basket," that is, who had charge of irrigating the land and preparing it for cultivation, are desperate. The Tigris waters do not rise, the river carries no good water.

> Famine was severe, nothing was produced,
> The small rivers *were not cleaned, the dirt was not carried off,*

On the steadfast fields no water was sprinkled, there was no
    digging of ditches,
In all the lands there were no *crops,* only weeds grew.
Thereupon the lord sets his lofty mind,
Ninurta, the son of Enlil, brings great things into being.

He sets up a heap of stones over the dead Kur and heaps
it up like a great wall in front of the land. These stones
hold back the "mighty waters" and as a result the waters
of the lower regions rise no longer to the surface of the
earth. As for the waters which had already flooded the
land, Ninurta gathers them and leads them into the Tigris,
which is now in a position to water the fields with its over-
flow. To quote the poet:

What had been scattered, he gathered,
What *by* Kur had been dissipated,
He guided and hurled into the Tigris,
The high waters it pours over the *farmland.*

Behold now everything on earth
Rejoiced afar at Ninurta, the king of the land;
The fields produced *much* grain,
The harvest of palm-grove and vineyard was fruitful,
It was heaped up in granaries and hills;
The lord made *mourning* disappear from the land,
He made good the liver of the gods.

Hearing of her son's great and heroic deeds, his mother
Ninmah—also known as Ninhursag and Nintu, and more
originally perhaps as Ki, the mother earth—is taken with
love for him; she becomes so restless that she is unable to
sleep in her bedchamber. She therefore addresses Ninurta
from afar with a prayer for permission to visit him and
feast her eyes upon him. Ninurta looks at her with the
"eye of life," saying:

"O thou lady, because thou wouldst come to a foreign land,
  O Ninmah, because for my sake thou wouldst enter an inimical
    land,
Because thou hast no fear of the terror of the battle surround-
    ing me,
Therefore, of the hill which I, the hero, have heaped up,
Let its name be Hursag (mountain), and thou be its queen."

Ninurta then blesses the Hursag that it may produce all kinds of herbs, wine and honey, various kinds of trees, gold, silver, and bronze, cattle, sheep, and all "four-legged creatures." After this blessing of the Hursag, he turns to the stones, cursing those which have been his enemies in his battle with Kur and blessing those which have been his friends; this entire passage, in style and tone, *not in content,* is very reminiscent of the blessing and cursing of Jacob's sons in the forty-ninth chapter of Genesis. The poem closes with a long hymnal passage exalting Ninurta.

The third version of the slaying-of-the-dragon myth is a poem consisting of one hundred and ninety lines of text which may be best entitled "Inanna and Ebih." [77] Although by 1934 eight pieces belonging to the story [78] had already been copied and published by the late Edward Chiera and Stephen Langdon, so little was understood of the myth that several of the pieces were not even recognized as belonging to it. A thorough reexamination of the material, including four hitherto unknown pieces, two from Istanbul and two from Philadelphia,[79] enabled me to reconstruct the major part of the text in the course of the past two years.

The dragon-slayer in this version of the story is not a god but a goddess, none other than Inanna, the counterpart of the Semitic Ishtar. For curious as it may seem, Inanna, to judge from our literary material, was conceived not only as the goddess of love but also as the goddess of battle and strife. And the reason for one of the puzzling and enigmatic epithets regularly ascribed to Inanna in the hymns, namely, "destroyer of Kur," is now clear. In our myth, it must be noted, Kur is also called "mountain Ebih," a district northeast of Sumer. This Kur represents, therefore, an inimical land, and is not to be identified with the cosmic Kur of the Ninurta and Enki versions.

The poem begins with a long hymnal passage extolling the virtues of Inanna. Follows a long address by Inanna to An, the heaven-deity, nominally, at least, the leading deity of the Sumerian pantheon (actually by the third millennium B. C. Enlil, the air-god, had already usurped his place). While the meaning of her speech is at times difficult to penetrate, Inanna's demand is clear; unless Kur, which seems quite unaware of, or at least oblivious to, her might and power, becomes duly submissive and is ready to glorify her virtues, she will do violence to the monster. To quote but part of her threat:

> "The long spear I shall hurl upon it,
> The throw-stick, the weapon, I shall direct against it,
> At its neighboring forests I shall strike up fire,
> At its . . . I shall set up the bronze ax,
> All its waters like Gibil (the fire-god) the purifier I shall dry up,
> Like the mountain Aratta, *I shall remove its dread,*
> Like a city cursed by An, it will not be restored,
> Like (a city) on which Enlil frowns, it shall not rise up."

An answers her with a detailed account of the mischief which Kur has wrought against the gods:

> "Against the standing place of the gods it has directed its terror,
> In the sitting place of the Anunnaki it has led forth fearfulness,
> Its dreadful fear it has hurled upon the land,
> The 'mountain,' its dreadful rays of fire it has directed against all the lands."

Continuing with a description of the power and wealth of Kur, An warns Inanna against attacking it. But Inanna is not taken aback by An's discouraging speech. Full of anger and wrath she opens the "house of battle" and leads out all her weapons and aids. She attacks and destroys Kur, and stationing herself upon it, she utters a paean of self-glorification.

INANNA'S DESCENT TO THE NETHER WORLD[11]

The text of this myth, which I have designated as "Inanna's Descent to the Nether World," has been reconstructed and deciphered by me in the course of the past six years. Its influence on literature and mythology has been universal and profound. Moreover, the story of its decipherment furnishes a most illuminating illustration of the not uninteresting process involved in the reconstruction of the texts of the Sumerian literary compositions.

For many years, for almost three-quarters of a century, a myth usually designated as "Ishtar's Descent to the Nether World" has been known to scholar and layman. Like the Babylonian "Epic of Creation," this poem was found inscribed in the Accadian language on tablets dating from the first millennium B. C.; these, therefore, postdate our Sumerian literary tablets by more than a millennium. Like the "Epic of Creation," "Ishtar's Descent to the Nether World," too, was therefore generally assumed to be of Semitic origin; it is cited and quoted in the major works concerned with mythology and religion as a remarkable example of Babylonian myth-making. With the appearance of the publications devoted to the Nippur material, however, it became gradually obvious that this "Semitic" myth goes back to a Sumerian original in which Ishtar is replaced by

---

PLATE XX. INANNA'S DESCENT TO THE NETHER WORLD

The 14 tablets and fragments illustrated here furnish a historical commentary on the reconstruction and translation of the myth "Inanna's Descent to the Nether World," recently published by the author.[80] The arrangement of the plate is aimed to illustrate the process of piecing together the tablets and fragments utilized in the reconstruction of the poem. Nos. 1, 2, and 5 were published by Poebel in 1914.[81] Nos. 3 and 4 were published by Langdon in 1914.[82] No. 6, which is in the University Museum, was identified by Chiera as the lower half of the very same tablet whose upper half, no. 3 on our plate, had been copied by Langdon in Istanbul. Chiera's discovery enabled me to publish my first reconstruction of the myth in 1937.[83] Nos. 7–9 were published by Chiera in 1934.[84] Nos. 10–12 were identified and copied by the author some five years ago in the Museum of the Ancient Orient at Istanbul.[85] Nos. 13 and 14 were identified and copied by the author recently in Philadelphia.[86] The utilization of these five newly discovered texts made possible the edition published in 1942. The marked passage on no. 8 contains the lines describing Inanna's decision to descend to the nether world; that on no. 13 contains the lines describing the death of the goddess; the reverse of no. 10 (not on our plate, which contains the obverse only) has the resurrection passage. The transliteration and the translation of these three most significant passages will be found in note 87.

(This plate is arranged from *Proceedings of the American Philosophical Society* 85 (3), plates 1–10.)

PLATE XX

INANNA'S DESCENT TO THE NETHER WORLD

(For description, see opposite page.)

Inanna, her Sumerian counterpart. Arno Poebel, now of the Oriental Institute of the University of Chicago, was the first to locate three small pieces belonging to this myth in the University Museum at Philadelphia; these were published as early as 1914.[81] In the very same year, the late Stephen Langdon, of Oxford, published two pieces which he had uncovered in the Museum of the Ancient Orient at Istanbul.[82] One of these was the upper half of a large four-column tablet which, as will soon become evident, proved to be of major importance for the reconstruction of the text of the myth. The late Edward Chiera uncovered three additional pieces in the University Museum. These were published in his two posthumous volumes consisting of copies of Sumerian literary texts which I prepared for publication for the Oriental Institute in 1934.[84]

By this time, therefore, we had eight pieces, all more or less fragmentary, dealing with the myth. Nevertheless the contents remained obscure, for the breaks in the tablets were so numerous and came at such crucial points in the story that an intelligent reconstruction of the extant parts of the myth remained impossible. It was a fortunate and remarkable discovery of Chiera which saved the situation. He discovered in the University Museum at Philadelphia, the *lower* half of the very same four-column tablet whose *upper* half had been found and copied by Langdon years before in the Museum of the Ancient Orient at Istanbul. The tablet had evidently been broken before or during the excavation, and the two halves had become separated; the one had been retained in Istanbul, and the other had come to Philadelphia. Unfortunately, Chiera, who fully realized the significance of his discovery, died before he was in a position to utilize it.

It was by making use of this lower half of the four-column tablet, despite the fact that it, too, is very poorly preserved, that I was enabled to reconstruct the contents of the myth. For when the two halves of the tablet were joined, the combined text furnished an excellent framework in which and about which all the other extant fragments could be properly arranged. Needless to say, there were still numerous gaps and breaks in the text which made the translation and interpretation of the text no easy matter, and the meaning of several of the more significant passages in the story remained obscure. In 1937 I was fortunate enough to discover in Istanbul three additional pieces belonging to the myth,[85] and upon returning to the United States in 1939 I located another large piece in the University Museum at Philadelphia, and yet another in 1940.[86] These three fragments helped to fill in the most serious lacunae in my first reconstruction and translation, and as a result, the myth, as far as it goes, is now almost complete; the scientific edition, including the original text, and its transliteration and translation, has just been published.[80]

Inanna, queen of heaven, the goddess of light and love and life, has set her heart upon visiting the nether world, perhaps in order to free her lover Tammuz. She gathers together all the appropriate divine decrees, adorns herself with her queenly robes and jewels, and is ready to enter the "land of no return." Queen of the nether world is her elder sister and bitter enemy Ereshkigal, the goddess of darkness and gloom and death. Fearing lest her sister put her to death in the nether world, Inanna instructs her messenger, Ninshubur, who is always at her beck and call, that if after three days she shall have failed to return, he is to go to heaven and set up a hue and cry for her in the assembly hall of the gods. Moreover, he is to go to Nippur, the very city where our tablets have been excavated, and there weep and plead before the god Enlil to save Inanna from Ereshkigal's clutches. If Enlil should refuse, he is to go to Ur, Ur of the Chaldees, whence according to Biblical tradition Abraham migrated to Palestine, and there repeat his plea before Nanna, the great Sumerian moongod. If Nanna, too, refuses, he is to go to Eridu, the city in which Sumerian civilization is said to have originated, and weep and plead before Enki, the "god of wisdom." And the latter, "who knows the food of life, who knows the water of life," will restore Inanna to life.

Having taken these precautions, Inanna descends to the nether world and approaches Ereshkigal's temple of lapis lazuli. At the gate she is met by the chief gatekeeper, who demands to know who she is and why she came. Inanna concocts a false excuse for her visit, and the gatekeeper, upon instructions from his mistress Ereshkigal, leads her through the seven gates of the nether world. As she passes through each of the gates part of her robes and jewels are removed in spite of her protest. Finally after entering the last gate she is brought stark naked and on bended knees before Ereshkigal and the seven Anunnaki, the dreaded judges of the nether world. These latter fasten upon Inanna their "look of death," whereupon she is turned into a corpse and hung from a stake.

So pass three days and three nights. On the fourth day, Ninshubur, seeing that his mistress has not returned, proceeds to make the rounds of the gods in accordance with his instructions. As Inanna had foreseen, both Enlil of Nippur and Nanna of Ur refuse all help. Enki, however, devises a plan to restore her to life. He fashions the *kurgarru* and *kalaturru,* two sexless creatures, and entrusts to them the "food of life" and the "water of life," with instructions to proceed to the nether world and to sprinkle this food and this water sixty times upon Inanna's suspended corpse. This they do and Inanna revives. As she leaves the nether world, however, to reascend to the earth, she is accompanied by the shades of the dead and by the bogies and harpies who have their home there. Surrounded by this ghostly, ghastly crowd, she wanders through Sumer from city to city.

Here all extant source material for "Inanna's Descent to the Nether World" unfortunately breaks off, but this is not the end of the myth. It is not too much to hope, however, that some day in the not too distant future the pieces on which the conclusion of the story is inscribed will be discovered and deciphered. Following is a literal translation of the composition; even in its present incomplete state it provides an excellent illustration of the mood and temper, the swing and rhythm of Sumerian poetry:

> From the "great above" she set her mind toward the "great below,"
>
> The *goddess,* from the "great above" she set her mind toward the "great below,"
>
> Inanna, from the "great above" she set her mind toward the "great below."

> My lady abandoned heaven, abandoned earth,
>   To the nether world she descended,
> Inanna abandoned heaven, abandoned earth,
>   To the nether world she descended,
> Abandoned lordship, abandoned ladyship,
>   To the nether world she descended.

> In Erech she abandoned Eanna,
>   To the nether world she descended,
> In Badtibira she abandoned Emushkalamma,
>   To the nether world she descended,
> In Zabalam she abandoned Giguna,
>   To the nether world she descended,
> In Adab she abandoned Esharra,
>   To the nether world she descended,
> In Nippur she abandoned Baratushgarra,
>   To the nether world she descended,
> In Kish she abandoned Hursagkalamma,
>   To the nether world she descended,
> In Agade she abandoned Eulmash,
>   To the nether world she descended.

> The seven divine decrees she fastened at the side,
> She sought out the divine decrees, placed them at her hand,
> *All the decrees she set up at (her) waiting foot,*
> The *shugurra,* the crown of the plain, she put upon her head,
> *Radiance* she placed upon her countenance,
> The . . . rod of lapis lazuli she gripped in (her) hand,
> Small lapis lazuli stones she tied about her neck,
> *Sparkling* . . . stones she fastened to her breast,
> A gold ring she gripped in her hand,
> A . . . breastplate she bound about her breast,
> All the garments of ladyship she *arranged* about her body,
> . . . *ointment* she put on her face.

Inanna walked toward the nether world,
Her messenger Ninshubur walked at her *side,*
The pure Inanna says to Ninshubur:
"O (thou who art) my constant support,
My messenger of favorable words,
My carrier of supporting words,
I am now descending to the nether world.

"When I shall have come to the nether world,
Fill heaven *with complaints for me,*
In the assembly shrine *cry out* for me,
In the house of the gods *rush about* for me,
Lower thy eye for me, *lower* thy mouth for me,
With . . . *lower* thy great . . . for me,
Like a pauper in a single garment dress for me,
To the Ekur, the house of Enlil, all alone direct thy step.

"Upon thy entering the Ekur, the house of Enlil,
Weep before Enlil:
'O father Enlil, let not thy daughter be *put to death* in the nether
    world,
Let not thy good metal be *ground up* into the dust of the nether
    world,
Let not thy good lapis lazuli be *broken up* into the stone of the
    stone-worker,
Let not thy *boxwood* be *cut up* into the wood of the wood-
    worker,
Let not the maid Inanna be *put to death* in the nether world.'

"If Enlil stands not by thee in this matter, go to Ur.

"In Ur upon thy entering the house of the . . . of the land,
The Ekishshirgal, the house of Nanna,
Weep before Nanna:
'O Father Nanna, let not thy daughter be *put to death* in the
    nether world,
Let not thy good metal be *ground up* into the dust of the nether
    world,
Let not thy good lapis lazuli be *broken up* into the stone of the
    stone-worker,
Let not thy *boxwood* be *cut up* into the wood of the wood-
    worker,
Let not the maid Inanna be put to death in the nether world.'

"If Nanna stands not by thee in this matter, go to Eridu.

"In Eridu upon thy entering the house of Enki,
Weep before Enki:
'O father Enki, let not thy daughter be *put to death* in the
    nether world,
Let not thy good metal be *ground up* into the dust of the nether
    world,
Let not thy good lapis lazuli be *broken up* into the stone of the
    stone-worker,
Let not thy *boxwood* be *cut up* into the wood of the wood-
    worker,
Let not the maid Inanna be *put to death* in the nether world.'

"Father Enki, the lord of wisdom,
Who knows the food of life, who knows the water of life,
He will surely bring me to life."

Inanna walked toward the nether world,
To her messenger Ninshubur she says:
"Go, Ninshubur,
The word which I have commanded thee . . ."

When Inanna had arrived at the lapis lazuli palace of the
    nether world,
At the door of the nether world she acted evilly,
In the palace of the nether world she spoke evilly:
"Open the house, gatekeeper, open the house,
Open the house, Neti, open the house, all alone I would enter."

Neti, the chief gatekeeper of the nether world,
Answers the pure Inanna:
"Who pray art thou?"

"I am the queen of heaven, the place where the sun rises."

"If thou art the queen of heaven, the place where the sun rises,
Why pray hast thou come to the land of no return?
On the road whose traveller returns not how has thy heart led
    thee?"

The pure Inanna answers him:
"My elder sister Ereshkigal,
Because her husband, the lord Gugalanna, had been killed,
To witness the funeral rites,
. . .; so be it."

Neti, the chief gatekeeper of the nether world,
Answers the pure Inanna:
"*Stay*, Inanna, to my queen let me speak,
To my queen Ereshkigal let me speak . . . let me speak."

Neti, the chief gatekeeper of the nether world,
Enters the house of his queen Ereshkigal and says to her:
"O my queen, a maid,
Like a god . . . ,
The door . . . ,
. . . ,
In Eanna . . . ,
The seven divine decrees she has fastened at the side,
She has sought out the divine decrees, has placed them at her
    hand,
All the decrees she has set up at (*her*) *waiting foot,*
The *shugurra,* the crown of the plain, she has put upon her
    head,
Radiance she has placed upon her countenance,
The . . . rod of lapis lazuli she has gripped in (her) hand,
Small lapis lazuli stones she has tied about her neck,
Sparkling . . . stones she has fastened to her breast,
A gold ring she has gripped in her hand,
A . . . breastplate she has bound about her breast,
All her garments of ladyship she has *arranged* about her body,
. . . *ointment* she has put on her face."

Then Ereshkigal . . . ,
Answers Neti, her chief gatekeeper:
"Come, Neti, chief gatekeeper of the nether world,
Unto the word which I command thee, give ear.
Of the seven gates of the nether world, open their locks,
Of the gate Ganzir, the 'face' of the nether world, define its
    rules;
Upon her (Inanna's) entering,
Bowed low . . . let her . . ."

Neti, the chief gatekeeper of the nether world,
Honored the word of his queen.
Of the seven gates of the nether world, he opened their locks,
Of the gate Ganzir, the 'face' of the nether world, he defined
    its rules.
To the pure Inanna he says:
"Come, Inanna, enter."

Upon her entering the first gate,
The *shugurra,* the "crown of the plain" of her head, was re-
    moved.
"What, pray, is this?"
"Extraordinarily, O Inanna, have the decrees of the nether world
    been perfected,
O Inanna, *do not question* the rites of the nether world."

Upon her entering the second gate,
The . . . rod of lapis lazuli was removed.
"What, pray, is this?"
"Extraordinarily, O Inanna, have the decrees of the nether world
     been perfected,
     O Inanna, *do not question* the rites of the nether world."

Upon her entering the third gate,
The small lapis lazuli stones of her neck were removed.
"What, pray, is this?"
"Extraordinarily, O Inanna, have the decrees of the nether world
     been perfected,
     O Inanna, *do not question* the rites of the nether world."

Upon her entering the fourth gate,
The sparkling . . . stones of her breast were removed.
"What, pray, is this?"
"Extraordinarily, O Inanna, have the decrees of the nether world
     been perfected,
     O Inanna, *do not question* the rites of the nether world."

Upon her entering the fifth gate,
The gold ring of her hand was removed.
"What, pray, is this?"
"Extraordinarily, O Inanna, have the decrees of the nether world
     been perfected,
     O Inanna, *do not question* the rites of the nether world."

Upon her entering the sixth gate,
The . . . breastplate of her breast was removed.
"What, pray, is this?"
"Extraordinarily, O Inanna, have the decrees of the nether world
     been perfected,
     O Inanna, *do not question* the rites of the nether world."

Upon her entering the seventh gate,
All the garments of ladyship of her body were removed.
"What, pray, is this?"
"Extraordinarily, O Inanna, have the decrees of the nether world
     been perfected,
     O Inanna, *do not question* the rites of the nether world."

Bowed low . . .

The pure Ereshkigal seated herself upon her throne,
The Anunnaki, the seven judges, pronounced judgment before
     her,
They fastened (their) eyes upon her, the eyes of death,

At their word, the word which tortures the spirit,

. . . ,

The sick woman was turned into a *corpse,*

The *corpse* was hung from a *stake.*

After three days and three nights had passed,

Her messenger Ninshubur,

Her messenger of favorable words,

Her carrier of supporting words,

Fills the heaven *with complaints for her,*

Cried for her in the assembly shrine,

Rushed about for her in the house of the gods,

Lowered his eye for her, *lowered* his mouth for her,

With . . . he *lowered* his great . . . for her,

Like a pauper in a single garment he dressed for her,

To the Ekur, the house of Enlil, all alone he directed his step.

Upon his entering the Ekur, the house of Enlil,

Before Enlil he weeps:

"O father Enlil, let not thy daughter be *put to death* in the nether world,

Let not thy good metal be *ground up* into the dust of the nether world,

Let not thy good lapis lazuli be *broken up* into the stone of the stone-worker,

Let not thy *boxwood* be *cut up* into the wood of the wood-worker,

Let not the maid Inanna be *put to death* in the nether world."

Father Enlil answers Ninshubur:

"My daughter, in the 'great above' . . . , in the 'great below' . . . ,

Inanna, in the 'great above' . . . , in the 'great below' . . . ,

The decrees of the nether world, the . . . decrees, to their place . . . ,

Who, pray, *to* their place . . .?"

Father Enlil stood not by him in this matter, he went to Ur.

In Ur upon his entering the house of the . . . of the land,

The Ekishshirgal, the house of Nanna,

Before Nanna he weeps:

"O father Nanna, let not thy daughter be *put to death* in the nether world,

Let not thy good metal be *ground up* into the dust of the nether world,

Let not thy good lapis lazuli be *broken* up into the stone of the stone-worker,

Let not thy *boxwood* be *cut up* into the wood of the wood-worker,

Let not the maid Inanna be *put to death* in the nether world."

Father Nanna answers Ninshubur:

"My daughter in the 'great above' . . . , in the 'great below' . . . ,

Inanna, in the 'great above' . . . , in the 'great below' . . . ,

The decrees of the nether world, the . . . decrees, to their place . . . ,

Who, pray, *to* their place . . .?"

Father Nanna stood not by him in this matter, he went to Eridu.

In Eridu upon his entering the house of Enki,

Before Enki he weeps:

"O father Enki, let not thy daughter be *put to death* in the nether world,

Let not thy good metal be *ground up* into the dust of the nether world,

Let not thy good lapis lazuli be *broken up* into the stone of the stone-worker,

Let not thy *boxwood* be *cut up* into the wood of the wood-worker,

Let not the maid Inanna be *put to death* in the nether world."

Father Enki answers Ninshubur:

"What now has my daughter done! I am troubled,

What now has Inanna done! I am troubled,

What now has the queen of all the lands done! I am troubled,

What now has the hierodule of heaven done! I am troubled."

. . . *he brought forth dirt* (and) fashioned the *kurgarru*,

. . . *he brought forth dirt* (and) fashioned the *kalaturru*,

To the *kurgarru* he gave the food of life,

To the .*kalaturru* he gave the water of life,

Father Enki says to the *kalaturru* and *kurgarru*:

. . . (nineteen lines destroyed)

"*Upon the corpse hung from a stake direct the fear of the rays of fire*,

Sixty times the food of life, *sixty times* the water of life, sprinkle upon it,

Verily Inanna will arise."

. . . (twenty-four(?) lines destroyed)

Upon the corpse hung from a stake they directed the fear of
  the rays of fire,
Sixty times the food of life, *sixty times* the water of life, they
  sprinkled upon it,
Inanna arose.

Inanna ascends from the nether world,
The Anunnaki fled,
(And) whoever of the nether world that had descended peace-
  fully to the nether world;
When Inanna ascends from the nether world,
Verily the dead *hasten ahead of her.*

Inanna ascends from the nether world,
The small *demons* like . . . reeds,
The large demons like tablet styluses,
Walked at her side.
Who walked in front of her, being without . . . , held a staff
  in the hand,
Who walked at her side, being without . . . , carried a weapon
  on the loin.
They who *preceded* her,
They who *preceded* Inanna,
(Were beings who) know not food, who know not water,
Who eat not sprinkled flour,
Who drink not libated *wine,*
Who take away the wife from the loins of man,
Who take away the child from the breast of the nursing mother.

Inanna ascends from the nether world;
Upon Inanna's ascending from the nether world,
Her messenger Ninshubur threw himself at her feet,
Sat in the dust, dressed in *dirt.*
The demons say to the pure Inanna:
"O Inanna, *wait before* thy city, *we would bring him to thee.*"

The pure Inanna answers the demons:
"(He is) my messenger of favorable words,
My carrier of supporting words,
He *fails* not my directions,
He delays not my commanded word,
He *fills* heaven *with complaints for me,*
In the assembly shrine he cried out for me,
In the house of the gods he rushed about for me,
He *lowered* his eye for me, he *lowered* his mouth for me,
With . . . he *lowered* his great . . . for me,

Like a pauper in a single garment he dressed for me,
To the Ekur, the house of Enlil,
In Ur, to the house of Nanna,
In Eridu, to the house of Enki (he directed his step),
He brought me to life."

"Let us *precede* her, in Umma to the Sigkurshagga let us precede
  her."

In Umma, from the Sigkurshagga,
Shara threw himself at her feet,
Sat in the dust, dressed in *dirt*.
The demons say to the pure Inanna:
"O Inanna, *wait before* thy city, we would bring him to thee."

The pure Inanna answers the demons:
  (Inanna's answer is destroyed)

"Let us *precede* her, in Badtibira to the Emushkalamma let us
  precede her."

In Badtibira from the Emushkalamma,
. . . threw themselves at her feet,
Sat in the dust, dressed in *dirt*.
The demons say to the pure Inanna:
"O Inanna, *wait before* thy city, we would bring them to thee."

The pure Inanna answers the demons:
  (Inanna's answer destroyed; the end of the poem is wanting).

CHAPTER IV

MISCELLANEOUS MYTHS

THE DELUGE

That the Biblical deluge story is not original with the Hebrew redactors of the Bible has been known now for more than half a century—from the time of the discovery and decipherment of the eleventh tablet of the Semitic Babylonian "Epic of Gilgamesh." The Babylonian deluge myth itself, however, is of Sumerian origin. For in 1914 Arno Poebel published and carefully translated a fragment consisting of the lower third of a six-column Sumerian tablet in the Nippur collection of the University Museum, the larger part of whose contents is devoted to the deluge myth.[88] Unfortunately this fragment still remains unique and unduplicated; neither in Istanbul nor in Philadelphia have I succeeded in uncovering any material that might help to restore the broken part of its contents.[v]

The first part of the poem deals with the creation of man and animals and with the founding of the five antediluvian cities: Eridu, Badtibira, Larak, Sippar, and Shuruppak. For some reason—the passage involved is completely destroyed—the flood was decreed to wipe out man. But at least some of the gods seemed to regret this decision. It was probably the water-god Enki, however, who contrived to save mankind. He informed Ziusudra, the Sumerian counterpart of the Biblical Noah, a pious, god-fearing, and humble king, of the dreadful decision of the gods and advised him to save himself by building a very large boat. The long passage giving the details of the construction of the boat is destroyed; when our text begins again it is in the midst of describing the flood:

> All the windstorms, exceedingly powerful, attacked as one,
> The deluge raged over *the surface of the earth*.

> After, for seven days and seven nights,
> The deluge had raged in the land,
> And the huge boat had been tossed about on the great waters,
> Utu came forth, who sheds light on heaven and earth.
> Ziusudra opened *a window* of the huge boat,
> Ziusudra, the king,
> Before Utu prostrated himself,
> The king kills an ox, slaughters a sheep.

Again a long break follows; when our text becomes intelligible once more, it is describing the immortalizing of Ziusudra:

> Ziusudra, the king,
> Before An and Enlil prostrated himself;
> Life like a god they give him,
> Breath eternal like a god they *bring down* for him.

> In those days, Ziusudra, the king,
> *The preserver of the name of . . . and* man,
> In the mountain *of crossing,* the mountain of Dilmun, the place where the sun rises,
> They (An and Enlil) caused to dwell.

The remainder of the poem is destroyed.

THE MARRIAGE OF MARTU [w]

As yet we have but one tablet inscribed with the text of this poem; it is in the Nippur collection of the University Museum and has been copied and translated in part by

---

Fig. 2. The Deluge

This figure gives the obverse and the reverse of the deluge tablet as published by Poebel in 1914.[88] The marked passage contains the lines describing the flood and reads as follows:

> *1. tu$_{15}$-ḫul-tu$_{15}$-ḫul-ni-gur$_4$-gur$_4$-gál dù-a-bi ur-bi ì-súg-gi-eš*
> *2. a-ma-ru ugu-kab-dug$_4$-ga ba-an-da-ab-ùr-ùr*
> *3. u$_4$-7-àm giš-7-àm*
> *4. a-ma-ru kalam-ma ba-ùr-ra-ta*
> *5. ^{giš}má-gur$_4$-gur$_4$ a-gal-la tu$_{15}$-ḫul-bul-bul-a-ta*
> *6. ^{d}utu im-ma-ra-è an-ki-a u$_4$-gá-gá*

For the translation, see pages 97–98.

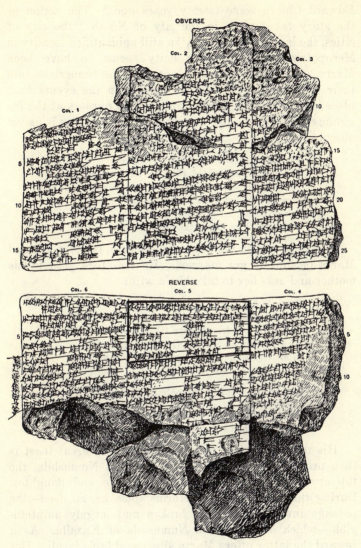

OBVERSE

COL. 2

COL. 1   COL. 3

5   10

15

10   20

15   25

REVERSE

COL. 6   COL. 5   COL. 4

5   5

10

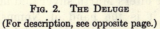

Fig. 2. The Deluge
(For description, see opposite page.)

Edward Chiera some twenty years ago.[89] The action of
the story takes place in the city of Ninab, "the city of
cities, the land of princeship," a still unidentified locality in
Mesopotamia. Its tutelary deity seems to have been
Martu, a west-Semitic god adopted by the Sumerians into
their pantheon. The relative time when the events took
place is described in laconic, antithetical phrases at the beginning of the poem, phrases whose exact meaning is as yet
obscure:

> Ninab existed, Shittab did not exist,
> The pure crown existed, the pure tiara did not exist,
> The pure herbs existed, the pure cedar trees did not exist,
> Pure salt existed, pure *nitrum* did not exist,
> Cohabitation . . . existed,
> In the meadows there was *birth-giving*.

For some reason not altogether clear in the text, the god
Martu decides to get married. He therefore goes to his
mother and asks her to take him a wife:

> Martu to his mother,
> Into the house enters, says:
> "In my city my friends have taken wives unto themselves,
> My neighbors have taken wives unto themselves,
> In my city I (alone) of my friends have no wife,
> Have no wife, have no child."

The remainder of the speech is obscure; it ends with:

> "O my mother, take for me a wife,
> *My gifts* I shall bring to thee."

His mother advises him accordingly. A great feast is
then prepared in Ninab, and to it comes Numushda, the
tutelary deity of Kazallu, with his wife and daughter.
During this feast Martu performs some heroic deed—the
passage involved is partly broken and largely unintelligible—which brings joy to Numushda of Kazallu. As a
reward the latter offers Martu silver and lapis lazuli. But
Martu refuses; it is the hand of Numushda's daughter
which he claims as his reward. Numushda gladly consents;
so, too, does his daughter, although an effort is made by

one of her close relatives to disparage Martu in her eyes as a crude barbarian:

> "Uncooked meat he eats,
>   During his life he has no house,
>   When he dies he lies unburied,
>   O my . . . , why wouldst thou marry Martu?"

To this argument Numushda's daughter answers simply: "Martu I shall marry," and our poem ends.

INANNA PREFERS THE FARMER [x]

This charming agricultural myth,[90] which I have entitled "Inanna Prefers the Farmer," is another example of the Cain-Abel motif. The characters of our poem are four in number: the seemingly ubiquitous Inanna; her brother, the sun-god Utu; the shepherd-god Dumuzi; the farmer-god Enkimdu. The plot is as follows. Inanna is about to choose a spouse. Her brother Utu urges her to marry the shepherd-god Dumuzi, but she prefers the farmer-god Enkimdu. Thereupon Dumuzi steps up and demands to know why she prefers the farmer; he, Dumuzi, the shepherd, has everything that the farmer has and more. Inanna does not answer, but Enkimdu, the farmer, who seems to be a peaceful, cautious type, tries to appease the belligerent Dumuzi. The latter refuses to be appeased, however, until the farmer promises to bring him all kinds of gifts and—here it must be stressed the meaning of the text is not quite certain—even Inanna herself.

The intelligible part of the poem begins with an address by the sun-god Utu to his sister Inanna:

> "O my sister, the much possessing shepherd,
>   O maid Inanna, why dost thou not favor?
>   His oil is good, his date-wine is good,
>   The shepherd, everything his hand touches is bright,
>   O Inanna, the much-possessing Dumuzi . . . ,
>   *Full of jewels* and precious stones, why dost thou not favor?
>   His good oil he will eat with thee,
>   The *protector* of the king, why dost thou not favor?"

But Inanna refuses:

> "The much-possessing shepherd I shall not marry,
> In his new . . . I shall not *walk*,
> In his new . . . I shall *utter no praise*,
> I, the maid, the farmer I shall marry,
> The farmer who makes plants grow abundantly,
> The farmer who makes the grain grow abundantly."

A break of about twelve lines follows, in which Inanna continues to give the reasons for her preference. Then the shepherd-god Dumuzi steps up to Inanna, protesting her choice—a passage that is particularly remarkable for its intricately effective phrase-pattern:

> "The farmer more than I, the farmer more than I,
>   The farmer what has he more than I?
> If he gives me his black garment, I give him, the farmer, my black ewe,
> If he gives me his white garment, I give him, the farmer, my white ewe,
> If he pours me his first date-wine, I pour him, the farmer, my *yellow* milk,
> If he pours me his good date-wine, I pour him, the farmer, my *kisim*-milk,
> If he pours me his 'heart-turning' date-wine, I pour him, the farmer, my bubbling milk,
> If he pours me his *water-mixed* date-wine, I pour him, the farmer, my *plant*-milk,
> If he gives me his good portions, I give him, the farmer, my *nitirda*-milk,
> If he gives me his good bread, I give him, the farmer, my *honey*-cheese,
> If he gives me his small beans, I give him my small cheeses;
> More than he can eat, more than he can drink,
> I pour out for him much oil, I pour out for him much milk;
> More than I, the farmer, what has he more than I?"

Follow four lines whose meaning is not clear; then begins Enkimdu's effort at appeasement:

> "Thou, O shepherd, why dost thou start a quarrel?
> O shepherd, Dumuzi, why dost thou start a quarrel?
> Me with thee, O shepherd, me with thee why dost thou compare?
> Let thy sheep eat the grass of the earth,

In my meadowland let thy sheep *pasture,*
In the fields of Zabalam let them eat grain,
Let *all* thy *folds* drink the water of my river Unun."

But the shepherd remains adamant:

"I, the shepherd, at my marriage do not enter, O farmer, as my
friend,
O farmer, Enkimdu, as my friend, O farmer, as my friend, do
not enter."

Thereupon the farmer offers to bring him all kinds of gifts:

"Wheat I shall bring thee, beans I shall bring thee,
Beans of . . . I shall bring thee,
The maid Inanna *(and) whatever is pleasing* to thee,
The maid Inanna . . . I shall bring thee."

And so the poem ends, with the seeming victory of the
shepherd-god Dumuzi over the farmer-god Enkimdu.

CHAPTER V

REFERENCES AND NOTES

Following is a list of abbreviations used in the notes:

AO Musée du Louvre, Paris. Antiquités orientales. (Followed by catalogue number).

AOF *Archiv für Orientforschung* (Berlin, 1923–).

AOR *Archiv Orientální* (Prague, 1928–).

AS Oriental Institute of the University of Chicago. *Assyriological Studies* (Chicago, 1931–).

AS No. 10 Kramer, Samuel N. *Gilgamesh and the huluppu-tree* (1938).

AS No. 11 Jacobsen, Thorkild. *The Sumerian king list* (1939).

AS No. 12 Kramer, Samuel N. *Lamentation over the destruction of Ur* (1940).

ASKT Haupt, Paul. *Akkadische und sumerische Keilschrifttexte* (Leipzig, 1881–1882).

ATU *Altorientalische Texte und Untersuchungen*, ed. by Bruno Meissner (Leiden, 1916–).

BA *Beiträge zur Assyriologie und semitischen Sprachwissenschaft*, edited by P. Haupt and F. Delitzsch (Baltimore and Leipzig, 1890–1927).

BASOR *Bulletin of the American Schools of Oriental Research* (Baltimore, 1919–).

BE The Babylonian expedition of the University of Pennsylvania. Series A: *Cuneiform texts*, ed. by H. V. Hilprecht (Philadelphia, 1893–1914).

BE XXIX Radau, Hugo. *Sumerian hymns and prayers to god Nin-ib, from the temple library of Nippur* (1911).

BE XXXI Langdon, Stephen H. *Historical and religious texts from the temple library of Nippur* (1914).

BBI Barton, George A. *Miscellaneous Babylonian inscriptions* (New Haven, 1918–).

BL Langdon, Stephen H. *Babylonian liturgies* (Paris, 1913).

CBS Museum of the University of Pennsylvania. Catalogue of the Babylonian section. (Followed by number.) All CBS numbers listed in the notes are still unpublished.

CT British Museum. *Cuneiform texts from Babylonian tablets . . . in the British Museum* (London, 1896–).

GSG Poebel, Arno. *Grundzüge der sumerischen Grammatik* (Rostock, 1923).

HAV	Radau, Hugo. "Miscellaneous texts from the temple library of Nippur," in *Hilprecht anniversary volume* (Leipzig, 1909): 374–457.
HRETA	Nies, J. B., and C. E. Keiser. *Historical, religious, and economic texts and antiquities* (New Haven, 1920).
JAOS	*Journal of the American Oriental Society* (Boston, etc., 1849–).
JRAS	*Journal of the Royal Asiatic Society of Great Britain and Ireland* (London, 1834–).
K	British Museum. Kouyunjik collection. (Followed by catalogue number.)
KAR	Ebeling, Erich. *Keilschrifttexte aus Assur religiösen Inhalts* (Wissenschaftliche Veröffentlichungen der Deutsche Orient-Gesellschaft, Bd. 28, Heft 1–4, and Bd. 34, Heft 1–; Leipzig, 1919–).
KGV	Abel, L., and H. Winkler. *Keilschrifttexte zum Gebrauch bei Vorlesungen* (Berlin, 1890).
MVAG	*Mitteilungen der Vorderasiatisch-aegyptische Gesellschaft* (Berlin, 1896–1908; Leipzig, 1909–).
Ni	Asari atika müzeleri (Museum of the Ancient Orient), Istanbul. Nippur collection. (Followed by catalogue number.) All Ni numbers listed in the notes will be published in *SLTN*.
OECT	*Oxford editions of cuneiform texts* (London, 1923–).
OECT I	Langdon, Stephen H. *Sumerian and Semitic religious and historical texts* (London, 1923).
PBS	Museum of the University of Pennsylvania. *Publications of the Babylonian section* (Philadelphia, 1911–).
PBS I 1	Myhrman, David W. *Babylonian hymns and prayers* (1911).
PBS I 2	Lutz, Henry F. *Selected Sumerian and Babylonian texts* (1919).
PBS IV 1	Poebel, Arno. *Historical texts* (1914).
PBS V	Poebel, Arno. *Historical and grammatical texts* (1914).
PBS VI 1	Poebel, Arno. *Grammatical texts* (1914).
PBS X 1	Langdon, Stephen H. *Sumerian epic of paradise, the flood, and the fall of man* (1915).
PBS X 2	Langdon, S. H. *Sumerian liturgical texts* (1917).
PBS X 4	Langdon, S. H. *Sumerian liturgies and psalms* (1919).
PBS XII	Langdon, S. H. *Sumerian grammatical texts* (1917).
PBS XIII	Legrain, Leon. *Historical fragments* (1922).
PRAK	Genouillac, Henri de. *Premières recherches archéologiques à Kich* (2 vols.; Paris, 1924–1925).
R	Rawlinson, Sir Henry. *The cuneiform inscriptions of Western Asia* (5 vols.; London, 1861–1884; vol. 4, 2d ed., 1891).

RA   *Revue d'assyriologie et d'archéologie orientale* (Paris, 1884–).

SAK   Thureau-Dangin, François. *Die sumerischen und akkad-
            ischen Königsinschriften* (Leipzig, 1907).

SBH   Reisner, George A. *Sumerisch-babylonische Hymnen nach
            Thontafeln griechischer Zeit* (Berlin, 1896).

SEM   Chiera, Edward. *Sumerian epics and myths* (Oriental Insti-
            tute publications XV; Chicago, 1934).

SL   Kramer, Samuel N. "Sumerian literature," in *Proceedings
            of the American Philosophical Society* 85.293–323, 1942.

SLTN   Kramer, Samuel N. *Sumerian literary texts from Nippur in
            the Museum of the Ancient Orient* (to appear in the near
            future under the auspices of the American School of
            Oriental Research at Bagdad and the American Council
            of Learned Societies).

SRT   Chiera, Edward. *Sumerian religious texts* (Crozer Theo-
            logical Seminary. Babylonian publications I; Upland,
            Pa., 1924).

STVC   Chiera, Edward. *Sumerian texts of varied contents* (Orien-
            tal Institute publications XVI; Chicago, 1934).

TRS   Genouillac, Henri de. *Textes religieux sumériens du Louvre*,
            Tomes I–II (Musée du Louvre, Department des an-
            tiquités orientales, *Textes cunéiformes*, Tomes XV–XVI;
            Paris, 1930).

U   Joint Expedition of the British Museum and of the Museum
            of the University of Pennsylvania to Mesopotamia. Ur
            collection. (Followed by catalogue number.)

VS   Staatliche Museen, Berlin. *Vorderasiatische Sehriftdenk-
            mäler* (Leipzig, 1907–).

  VS II   Zimmern, Heinrich. *Sumerische Kultlieder aus altbabylon-
            ischer Zeit, 1. Reihe* (1912).

  VS X   Zimmern, Heinrich. *Sumerische Kultlieder aus altbabylon-
            ischer Zeit, 2. Reihe* (1913).

VAT   Staatliche Museen, Berlin. Tontafelsammlung, Vorder-
            asiatische Abteilung. (Followed by catalogue number.)

1. The extant text of this poem, which we may entitle "The Epic of
Enmerkar," is reconstructed from the following tablets and fragments:
CBS 29.13.194, 29.16.422; *PBS V* 8; *PBS XIII* 8; *SEM* 14, 16; *SRT* 34.
The following pieces may also belong to this composition: *BE XXXI* 44
(*cf.* Kramer, *JAOS* 60.250); CBS 2291, 7859; *HAV* 9. "The Epic of
Enmerkar" is to be kept distinct from another epic tale concerned with
the same Enmerkar, which we may entitle "Enmerkar and Enmushkesh-
danna." The extant text of the latter poem is reconstructed from the
following tablets and fragments: Ni 2283; *PBS V* 9, 10; *SEM* 13,18,19.
The following pieces also probably belong to it: CBS 29.16.450; *HAV* 17;
SEM 17. In *SL* 320 I assumed that we had but one epic composition

dealing with the exploits of Enmerkar in the course of subjugating Aratta to Erech. It now seems more likely that we actually have two such epic tales. The first, described in *SL* as the "larger portion," corresponds to the poem designated above as "The Epic of Enmerkar"; the second, described in *SL* as the "smaller portion," corresponds to the one designated "Enmerkar and Enmushkeshdanna." Note also that the number of pieces identified as belonging to these two poems is 20, not 25, as stated in *SL* 320.

2. The transliteration and translation of this passage are as follows:

1. *u₄-ba muš-nu-gál-la-àm gír nu-gál-la-àm[ka nu-gál-la-àm]*
2. *ur-maḫ nu-gál-la-àm ur-zir(?) ur-bar-ra nu-gál-la-am*
3. *ní-te-gá su-zi-zi-i nu-gál-la-àm*
4. *lú-lu₆ gaba-šu-gar nu-um-tuku-àm*
5. *u₄-ba kur-šubur ki-ḫé-me-zi*
6. *eme-ḫa-mun ki-en-gi kur-gal-me-nam-nun-na-kam*
7. *ki-uri kur-me-te-gál-la*
8. *kur-mar-tu-ú-sal-la-ná-a*
9. *an-ki-nigin-na uku-sag-sì-ga*
10. *ᵈen-líl-ra eme-aš-àm he-en-na-da-[si(?)-el(?)]*

In those days there was no snake, there was no scorpion, there was no *hyena,*
There was no lion, there was no *wild dog,* no wolf,
There was no fear, no terror,
Man had no rival.

In those days the land Shubur (East), the place of plenty, of righteous decrees,
Harmony-tongued Sumer (South), the great land of the "decrees of princeship,"
Uri (North), the land having all that is *needful,*
The land Martu (West), resting in security,
The whole universe, the people *in unison,*
To Enlil in one tongue *gave praise.*

3. The term Accadian is now generally applied to the Semitic language spoken in the countries commonly known as Assyria and Babylonia; Assyrian and Babylonian, the terms formerly used to designate this language, are the names of the two best-known dialects of the Accadian language.

4. No satisfactory history of Sumer and the Sumerians has as yet been written. However, the interested reader will obtain a relatively adequate orientation in respect to the fundamental pattern of Sumerian history and its basic problems by examining such works as: L. W. King, *A History of Sumer and Akkad* (London, 1910); *The Cambridge Ancient History,* Vol. I (1923; especially chapters X–XII by Stephen Langdon);

C. L. Wooley, *The Sumerians* (Oxford, 1929); E. A. Speiser, *Mesopotamian Origins: The Basic Population of the Near East* (Philadelphia, 1930); Henri Frankfort, *Archaeology and the Sumerian Problem* (Oriental Institute Studies in Ancient-Oriental Civilization, No. 4; Chicago, 1932); W. F. Albright, *From the Stone Age to Christianity* (Baltimore, 1940). The reader will find that the statements formulated in these volumes not infrequently show serious divergences, inconsistencies, and contradictions; he is asked to bear in mind that the pertinent source material is highly complex in character and that its study and interpretation are still in a continuous and progressive state of flux.

5. For a more detailed sketch of the decipherment of the cuneiform system of writing, *cf.* E. A. Wallis Budge, *The Rise and Progress of Assyriology* (London, 1925); the reader will also find here an excellent pertinent bibliography. For the decipherment of Sumerian in particular, *cf.* F. H. Weissbach, *Zur Lösung der Sumerischen Frage* (Leipzig, 1897). As a matter of historical curiosity it is noteworthy to mention that in spite of all evidence to the contrary, the well-known orientalist, J. Halévy, continued to deny the existence of a Sumerian people and language in Mesopotamia, as late as the first decade of the twentieth century. According to his biased and subjectively motivated views, no people other than the Semites had ever been in possession of Babylonia. As for the so-called Sumerian language, it was merely an artificial invention of the Semites, themselves, devised for hieratic and esoteric purposes.

6. The first forty thousand tablets were discovered by the Arab workers while De Sarzec, the excavator, happened to be away from the mound. They succeeded in getting them all into the hands of dealers, and as a result, there is no important collection in Europe or America which does not have some Lagash tablets. In the Museum of the Ancient Orient, the tablets excavated at Lagash in the course of the years are stacked high in drawer after drawer; it is difficult to estimate their number but it may be close to 100,000.

7. For a detailed description of the Nippur excavations, *cf.* J. P. Peters, *Nippur* (2 vols.; New York, 1897); H. V. Hilprecht, *The Excavations in Assyria and Babylonia* (The Babylonian expedition of the University of Pennsylvania, series D: *Researches and Treatises;* Philadelphia, 1904); C. S. Fischer, *Excavations at Nippur* (Berlin, 1907). The tablet material published to date has appeared largely in the two series *BE* and *PBS; cf. Orientalia* 27.9–10,13–14; to be added are *BBI, HAV, SEM, SRT, STVC;* also Leon Legrain, *Babylonian Inscriptions and Fragments from Nippur and Babylon* (*PBS XV*, 1926); Edward Chiera, *Sumerian Lexical Texts from the Temple School of Nippur* (Oriental Institute Publications XI; Chicago, 1929). For the seals and terra cottas from Nippur, *cf.* Leon Legrain, *The Culture of the Babylonians from Their Seals in the Collections of the Museum* (*PBS XIV*, 1925), and *Terra Cottas from Nippur* (*PBS XVI*, 1930).

8. For a detailed sketch of the excavations on Sumerian sites, *cf.* *Handbuch der Archäologie im Rahmen des Handbuchs der Altertumwissenschaft* I (ed. by Walter Otto; Munich, 1939), pp. 644 ff.; also Seton Lloyd, *Mesopotamian Excavations on Sumerian Sites* (London, 1936).

9. For a list of the large number of publications containing the Sumerian economic documents, *cf.* *Orientalia* 27.31–40, and the annual bibliographies in *AOF*.

10. The greater part of this material has been gathered, transliterated, and translated by the eminent French Assyriologist in his *SAK* as early as 1907; this volume is still basic and standard. The most significant addition to this material in recent days is C. J. Gadd and L. Legrain, *Royal Inscriptions* (Publications of the Joint Expedition of the British Museum and of the University Museum, University of Pennsylvania, to Mesopotamia. *Ur Excavations, Texts* I., London, 1928).

11. For a list of the publications, *cf.* *Orientalia* 27.31–40 and the annual bibliographies in *AOF*. The mathematical texts, especially, have now found ample treatment; *cf.* Thureau-Dangin (in RA 24–35) and Otto Neugebauer, *Mathematische Keilschrifttexte* (Berlin, 1935–1937).

12. The publications involved are *CT XV, CT XXXVI, OECT I, PRAK, TRS, VS II, VS X.* Small numbers of literary tablets are naturally to be found in other collections. The Yale Babylonian Collection, especially, as Professors Stephens and Goetze inform me, has accumulated quite a number of Sumerian literary tablets, bought from the hands of dealers. No doubt many of these were dug up in Nippur.

13. For a more detailed sketch of the Sumerian epics and myths, *cf.* *SL* 318–323.

14. A more detailed discussion of this material will be found in the introduction to *SLTN.*

15. *AS No 12.*

16. For the scientific analysis of the contents of the catalogue tablet, *cf.* Kramer, "Oldest Literary Catalogue," in *BASOR* 88.10–19.

17. Following are the major studies concerned with the origin and development of the cuneiform system of writing: F. Thureau-Dangin, *Recherches sur l'origine de l'ecriture cunéiforme* (Paris, 1898); G. A. Barton, *The Origin and Development of Babylonian Writing (BA IX)*; A. Deimel, *Liste der archäischen Keilschriftzeichen* (Wissenshaftliche Veröffentlichungen der Deutsche Orient-Gesellschaft, Bd. 40; Leipzig, 1922); E. Unger, *Die Keilschrift* (Leipzig, 1929); A. Falkenstein, *Archäische Texte aus Uruk* (Ausgrabungen der Deutschen Forschungsgemeinschaft in Uruk-Warka, Bd. 2; Leipzig, 1936).

18. If, proceeding from top to bottom, we examine the first column of the table (fig. 1), we note the following:

No. 1 is the picture of a star; it represents primarily the Sumerian word *an*, "heaven." The very same sign, however, is used to represent the word *dingir*, "god."

No. 2 represents the word *ki*, "earth." Obviously it is intended to be a picture of the earth, although the interpretation of the sign is still uncertain.

No. 3 is probably a more or less stylized picture of the upper part of a man's body; it represents the word *lu*, "man."

No. 4 is a picture of the pudenda; it represents the word *sal*, "pudenda." The same sign is used to represent the word *munus*, "woman."

No. 5 is the picture of a mountain; it represents the word *kur*, whose primary meaning is "mountain."

No. 6 illustrates an ingenious device developed early by the inventors of the Sumerian system of writing, whereby they were enabled to represent pictorially words for which the ordinary pictographic representation entailed a certain amount of difficulty. As the reader will note, the sign for the word *geme*, "slave-girl," is actually a combination of two signs, that for *munus*, "woman," and that for *kur*, "mountain"; that is, of signs 4 and 5 on our table. Literally, therefore, this compound sign expresses the idea "mountain-woman." But since the Sumerians obtained their slave-girls largely from the mountainous regions about them, this compound sign adequately represented the Sumerian word for "slave-girl," *geme*.

No. 7 is the picture of a head; it represents the Sumerian word *sag*, "head."

No. 8 is also the picture of a head; the vertical strokes, however, underline the particular part of the head which is intended, that is, the mouth. This sign, therefore, represents the Sumerian word *ka*, "mouth." The same sign naturally enough represents the word *dug*, "to speak."

No. 9 is probably the picture of a bowl used primarily as a food-container; it represents the word *ninda*, "food."

No. 10 is actually a compound sign consisting of the signs for mouth and food (nos. 8 and 9 on our table); it represents the word *ku*, "to eat."

No. 11 is a picture of a water stream; it represents the word *a*, "water." This sign furnishes an excellent illustration of the process by which the Sumerian script gradually lost its unwieldy pictographic character and became a phonetic system of writing. As just said, the sign no. 11 was used primarily to represent the Sumerian word *a*, "water." However, the Sumerians had another word *a* which was identical in pronunciation with the word *a*, "water," but which had the entirely different meaning "in." Now this word "in" is a word denoting relationship and stands for a concept which is very difficult to express pictographically. To the originators of the Sumerian script then came the ingenious idea that instead of trying to invent a necessarily highly complicated picture-sign to represent the word "in," they could use the sign for *a*, "water," since both words sounded exactly alike. In other words, the early Sumerian scribes came to realize that a sign originally belonging to a given word could be used for another word with an altogether unrelated meaning, if the *sound* of the two words were identical. With the gradual spreading of this practice, the Sumerian script lost its pictographic character and tended more and more to become a purely phonetic script.

No. 12 is a combination of the signs for "mouth" and "water" (nos. 8 and 11); it represents the word *nag*, "to drink."

No. 13 is a picture of the lower part of the leg and foot in walking position; it represents the word *du*, "to go," and also the word *gub*, "to stand."

No. 14 is a picture of a bird; it represents the word *mushen*, "bird."

No. 15 is a picture of a fish; it represents the word *ha*, "fish." This sign furnishes another example of the phonetic development of the Sumerian script. For the Sumerian word *ha* not only had the meaning "fish" but also "may"; that is, the Sumerians had two words *ha* which were identical in pronunciation but quite unrelated in meaning. And so, early in the development of the script the Sumerian scribes began to use the sign for *ha*, "fish," to represent the phonetically identical *ha*, "may," just as in the case of sign no. 11 they used the sign for *a*, "water," to represent the word *a*, "in."

No. 16 is a picture of the head and horns of an ox; it represents the word *gud*, "ox."

No. 17 is a picture of the head of a cow; it represents the word *ab*, "cow."

No. 18 is the picture of an ear of barley; it represents the word *še*, "barley."

The signs in the first column which we have examined in detail are from the earliest period in the development of Sumerian writing known to date. Not long after the invention of the pictographic script, however, the Sumerian scribes found it convenient to turn the tablet in such a way that the pictographs lay on their backs. As the writing developed, this practice became standard and the signs were regularly turned 90 degrees. The second column in our tablet gives the pictographic signs in this turned position. To judge from our present data and speaking very roughly, this pictographic script may be dated 3200–2800 B. C. The third column of our table represents what may be termed the "archaic" script, dated roughly 2800–2600 B. C. The fourth column contains the sign-forms of the classical period, 2600–2450 B. C.; the inscriptions of this period contain the purest Sumerian known to date. The Nippur archaic cylinder (plate III), inscribed with the oldest myth known, probably belongs to the very end of this period.

The fifth column contains the sign-forms of the Sargonid period, roughly 2450–2150 B. C.; it is in this period that the Sumerians met with serious defeats at the hands of the Semites and the Guti. A brief renaissance of Sumerian power followed in the Neo-Sumerian period, roughly 2150–2050 B. C. The sixth column represents the Sumerian script of this period. With the destruction of the city of Ur, about 2050 B. C., Sumer practically ceased to exist as a political entity. The period that followed, roughly 2050–1700 B. C., is known as the "early post-Sumerian." During this period Sumerian, though no longer a living language, was retained as the literary and religious language of the Semitic conquerors. It is in this period that by far the greater part of our source material was inscribed, though much of it may have been composed considerably earlier; the seventh column contains the sign-forms then used. The last column illustrates the script as used largely in the first millennium B. C. by the royal scribes of Assyria. It is primarily this late, highly conventionalized script which the European scholars of the nineteenth century first studied and deciphered. And illogically enough, to this very day, this is the script with which students of cuneiform begin their studies.

19. For an excellent copy of the text, cf. F. Thureau-Dangin, Les cylindres de Gudea, découverts par Ernest de Sarzec à Tello (Musée du Louvre, Departement des antiquités orientales, Textes cunéiformes, tome VIII; Paris, 1925); for the transliteration and translation, cf. SAK 88–141.

20. BBI 1.

21. For a discussion and bibliography, cf. Albright, From the Stone Age to Christianity, pp. 11 ff.

22. For a fuller comparative analysis of the Babylonian borrowings from Sumerian literature, cf. my review of A. Heidel, The Babylonian Genesis (Chicago, 1942), in the JAOS 63.69–73.

23. The Chicago Syllabary and the Louvre Syllabary AO 7661 (AS No. 7, 1940).

24. For a transliteration and translation of the text, together with a scientific analysis of its significance for Sumerian grammar, cf. PBS VI 1, pp. 29–53.

25. I. e. GSG. Cf. also the comment in SL. 320. As for the Sumerische Lesestücke which Poebel had prepared to accompany the grammar (cf. AOR 8.27, note 2; the hopes there expressed have not materialized), unfortunately these still remain unpublished.

26. A full discussion of the lexical problems will be found in my study, "The present status of Sumerian lexicology and lexicography," which, it is hoped, will be published in the near future.

27. These are SEM and STVC.

28. Cf. SL 320–323, and add "Inanna Prefers the Farmer" (see p. 100).

29. Edited by James Hastings. 13 vols.; Edinburgh, 1908–1927. Cf. the article, "Cosmogony and Cosmology," in volume 4, pp. 125–179.

30. Edited by L. H. Gray, J. A. MacCulloch, and G. F. Moore; Boston, 1916–1932. In volume IX, Semitic Mythology (1931), Stephen Langdon does make an attempt to sketch some of the Sumerian mythological concepts. However, because of the limited material available at

the time and because of the ubiquitous linguistic difficulties, much of the material there outlined is quite untrustworthy and misleading.

31. To date, however, it must be frankly admitted, relatively little of this glyptic material can be interpreted with any approach to certainty. Frequently we can neither identify the gods depicted on the designs, nor interpret even roughly the acts pictured and their implications. It is quite unlikely that, with the limited space and means at their disposal, the seal-cutters attempted to portray a connected story such as that told in "Gilgamesh, Enkidu, and the Nether World" or in "Inanna's Descent to the Nether World." And if, in order to overcome their limitations, they developed a system of abbreviation and conventionalization, we are not yet in a position to penetrate it. And so, in spite of the fact that so much intelligible Sumerian mythological material has now become available, very few of the cylinder seal designs can be identified with the stories told in our epics and myths. Nevertheless, as plates VI, IX, XI, XIII, and XVIII show, some of this glyptic material is most revealing and instructive. Except for the first two designs on plate XVIII, all the illustrations are taken from *Cylinder Seals*, a book recently published by Henri Frankfort, of the Oriental Institute of the University of Chicago, who is the leading living authority on the subject.

32. In detail these published texts are as follows: *BE XXXI* 35, 55 (*cf. JAOS* 60.246, 254; also *AS No. 11*, p. 89, note 128); *HAV* 11, 12; *SEM* 21, 22; *SRT* 39; U 9364 (= *RA* 30.127 ff.).

33. *GSG* p. 4.

34. *AS No. 10.*

35. These are CBS 10400, 15150, 29.13.438, 29.13.536, 29.15.993, 29.16.58, 29.16.463; Ni 4249.

36. *SEM* 21.

37. The Sumerian transliteration of these lines reads:

1. *an ki-ta ba-ra-bad-du-a-ba*
2. *ki an-ta ba-da-sur-ra-a-ba*
3. *mu-nam-lú-lu$_6$ ba-gar-ra-a-ba*
4. *u$_4$ an-ni an ba-an-ir$_{10}$-a-ba*
5. *^{d}en-líl-li ki ba-an-ir$_{10}$-a-ba*
6. *^{d}ereš-ki-gal-la kur-ra sag-rig$_7$-bi-šè im-ma-ab-rig$_7$-a-ba*

38. The text is copied by Langdon in *PBS X 4*, 16.

39. The Sumerian transliteration of these lines reads:

1. *en-e níg-du$_7$-e pa na-an-ga-àm-mi-in-è*
2. *en-nam-tar-ra-na-šu-nu-bal-e-dè*
3. *^{d}en-líl-numun-kalam-ma-ki-ta-e$_{11}$-dè*
4. *an ki-ta bad-du-dè sag na-an-ga-àm-ma-an-sì*
5. *ki an-ta bad-du-dè sag na-an-ga-àm-ma-an-sì*

40. The latter half of this Sumerian poem, translated almost verbatim into Accadian, is known as the *twelfth* tablet of the Babylonian "Epic of Gilgamesh"; our Sumerian poem clarifies this Accadian tablet, whose meaning has remained obscure for more than half a century. A full discussion of the problems involved will be found in the critical review of F. M. Th. Böhl, *Het Gilgamesj-Epos* (Amsterdam, 1941), which I am preparing for the *JAOS*.

41. *TRS* 10.36–37. Although treated in this list as the wife of An, her epithet *ama-tu-an-ki*, "the mother who gave birth to heaven and earth," reveals her original character. *Cf.* also *SEM* 116 i 16 (= TRS 71 i 16), where the goddess Nammu is described as *ama-palil-ù-tu-dingir-šár-šár-ra-ke₄-ne*, "the mother, the ancestress, who gave birth to all the gods."

42. For a comparative analysis of the Sumerian concepts of the creation of the universe and those revealed in the Semitic creation epic *Enuma elish*, *cf.* my comments in *JAOS* 63.69–73.

43. *Cf.* the Sin hymn restored from *SRT* 9 and *TRS* 21 (*JAOS* 60.412).

44. *Cf. HAV* 4.8–10. It is not improbable that *HAV* 4 is part of the epic tale "Lugalbanda and Mt. Hurrum" (*cf. SL* 321, No. 3); the other tablets and fragments belonging to this poem are CBS 7085, 29.16.228; *OECT I* pl. 19 (Stevenson tablet); *SEM* 20; *TRS* 90.

45. *Cf. SEM* 21.44–46 and its duplicate *SRT* 39.7–9; also *AS No. 10*, p. 5, 11.45–47, where line 47 is to be restored to read: *ᵈutu gán(?)-nun-ta e₁₁-da-a-ni*.

46. *Cf.* the tablet Kish 1932, 155 (*JRAS* 62.914–921) ii 2, which can be restored from its duplicates CBS 29.15.364 and 29.16.84 to read: *ᵈutu úr-ama-ni-ᵈnin-gal-la sag-íl-la mu-un-du*. All these texts are part of the epic tale "Gilgamesh and Huwawa" (*cf. SL* 321), a scientific edition of which I am now preparing.

47. *BBI* 4; note also the Pinches bilingual identified by Barton (*BBI* p. 34).

48. These are CBS 8176, 8315, 10309, 10322, 10412, 13853, 29.13.574, 29.15.611; Ni 2707. The following groups form "joins": CBS 8176 + 8315 + 13853; 10309 + 10412.

49. For the tablets and fragments utilized to reconstruct the text, *cf.* the two preceding notes.

50. The poem consists of approximately 313 lines of text reconstructed from the following tablets and fragments: *BL* 1; CBS 2244, 2284, 9804, 14026, 29.13.7, 29.13.189, 29.13.223, 29.15.35, 29.15.67, 291.15.74, 29.15.420, 29.15.650; Ni 3047, 4002; *SRT* 24; *STVC* 92. The following groups form "joins": 2244 + 29.15.420; 9804 + 29.15.35 + 29.15.74; 29.13.7 + 29.15.650.

51. The poem consists of approximately 308 lines of text reconstructed from the following tablets and fragments: *BBI* 7; CBS 3167, 10431, 13857, 29.13.464, 29.16.142, 29.16.232, 29.16.417, 29.16.427, 29.16.446, 29.16.448;

Ni 2705, 3167, 4004; *SEM* 46; *SRT* 41; *STVC* 125. The following groups form "joins": *BBI* 7 + 29.16.142; 13857 + 29.16.427 + 29.16.446 + 29.16.448.

52. *Cf. JAOS* 54.418 and *JAOS* 60.239, note 15. To the 11 tablets and fragments there listed, the following 9 are to be added: CBS 8531, 10310, 10335, 29.16.23, 29.16.436 (the number of unpublished pieces in the University Museum is therefore 5, not "at least 6" as stated in *JAOS* 60.239, note 15); Ni 1117, 2337, 2473, 2742 (2 fragments were identified by me after the publication of *JAOS* 60.239, note 15).

53. The poem consists of close to 200 lines of text reconstructed from the following tablets and fragments: *BBI* 8; *BE XXXI* 15; CBS 7344, 7916, 15161, 29.15.973; *HAV* 6; Ni 2308, 4036, 4094; *SEM* 38, 54, 55, 56, 57; *SRT* 25, 44. The following groups form "joins": CBS 7344 + 7916 + *SEM* 5 + *SEM* 77; CBS 29.15.973 + *SEM* 38. All in all, therefore, we now have 17 pieces belonging to the myth, and the statement in *SL* 322 no. 5 is to be modified accordingly (the number 9 there given resulted from the fact that the four fragments constituting the first "join" mentioned above were counted as one while the 5 pieces Ni 2308, 4036, 4044, *SEM* 38, and *SRT* 41 were not identified until after the publication of *SL*). The first 70 lines of the poem were transliterated and translated by Chiera in *SRT* pp. 26 ff.

54. *PBS X 1*, 1; *cf.* also Langdon, *Semitic Mythology*, chapter V.

55. *TRS* 62; *cf. JAOS* 54.417; obv. 1 and rev. 1 of this text correspond respectively to *PBS X 1*, 1 iii 21 and iv 43 (the two texts have a considerable number of variants).

56. The Sumerian transliteration of these lines reads:

1. ^{d}*nin-ḫur-sag-gá-ke₄ a-šà-ga ba-ni-in-ri*
2. *a-šà-ga šu ba-ni-in-ti a-^{d} en-ki-ga-ka*
3. *u₄-1-àm itu-1-a-ni*
4. *u₄-2-àm itu-2-a-ni*
5. *u₄-3-àm itu-3-a-ni*
6. *u₄-4-àm itu-4-a-ni*
7. *u₄-5-àm*
8. *u₄-6-àm*
9. *u₄-7-àm*
10. *u₄-8-àm*
11. *u₄-9-àm itu-9-a-ni nam-munus-a-ka*
12. *ià-?-gim ià-?-gim ià-dùg-nun-na-gim*
13. ^{d}*nin-tu ama-kalam-ka ià-?-gim*
14. ^{d}*nin-sar in-tu-ud*

57. For the tablets and fragments utilized in the reconstruction of its text, *cf.* the two preceding notes.

58. We may have here a prototype of the "forbidden fruit" motif of Genesis III.

59. The extant text of the poem is reconstructed from the following tablets and fragments: CBS 29.15.38; Ni 4006; *PBS X 2*, 1; *SRT* 44; *STVC* 78–80 (these three fragments form a "join"); *TRS* 36; *cf. JAOS* 54.413 and *SEM* p. 5, which are to be modified accordingly.

60. The poem consists of 128 lines of text reconstructed from the following tablets and fragments: *BE XXXI* 20; CBS 2167, 2216, 4916, 10314, 10350, 29.13.207, 29.15.337, 29.16.184, 29.16.251; *HRETA* 23; Ni 4031; *OECT I* pls. 1–4; *PBS I 2*, 105; *PBS X 2*, 20; *SEM* 81–85; *TRS* 54, 94. *Cf.* also *JAOS* 54.416; *JAOS* 60.242, note 26, where the number 6 should read 9; *SL* 322 no. 8, where the number 21 should read 22.

61. *PBS V* 25.

62. *PBS I 1*, 1.

63. Ni 4151.

64. Ni 2724.

65. The Sumerian transliteration of these lines reads:

1. *mu-á-mà mu-á-mà*
2. *kug-^{d}inanna-ra dumu-mu-úr ga-na-ab-sì* . . .
3. *nam-en nam-si nam-dingir aga-zi-maḫ ^{giš}gu-za-nam-lugal*
4. *kug-^{d}inanna-ke₄ šu ba-ti*
5. *mu-á-mà mu-á-mà*
6. *kug-^{d}inanna-ra dumu-mu-úr ga-na-ab-sì* . . .
7. *pa-maḫ ebur-šubur bara-maḫ nam-sibad nam-lugal*
8. *kug-^{d}inanna-ke₄ šu ba-ti*

66. The Sumerian transliteration of these lines reads:

1. *mu-á-mà mu-á-mà*
2. *kug-^{d}inanna-ra dumu-mu-úr ga-na-ab sì* . . .
3. *nam-nagar nam-tibira nam-dub-sar nam-sumug nam-ašgab nam-lú-? nam-dím nam-ad-ke₄*
4. *kug-^{d}inanna-ke₄ šu ba-ti*

67. In detail the reconstruction of the lines of the text is as follows (the line numbering is approximate): 1–3, broken; 4–30 = *PBS I 1*, 1 (= A) i; 31–50, broken; 51–65 = Ni 2724; 63–89 = A ii; 90–99, broken; 100–144, restored from repeated passages; 145–159 = A iii; 160–171, restored from repeated passages; 172–181, broken; 182–234, restored from repeated passages; 227–270 = A iv; 271–285, restored from repeated passages; 286–305, broken; 306–349 = A v; 350–367, restored from repeated passages; 368–391, broken; 392–402 = A vi; 403–413, broken; 413–421 = Ni 4151 obv.; 413–824 = *PBS V* 25.

68. *PBS X 4*, 14.

69. *SEM* 116.

70. CBS 2168.

71. The Sumerian transliteration of these lines reads:

1. *ama-ni(!) mud-mu-gar-ra-zu i-gál-la-àm ?-dingir-ri-e-ne
   kéš-da-i*
2. *šà-im-ugu-abzu-ka ù-mu-e-ni-šár*
3. *sig₇-en-sig₇-dùg im mu-e-gur₄-gur₄-ri-ne za-e me-GIM ù-me-
   ni-gál*
4. *ᵈnin-maḫ-e an-ta-zu ḫé-ag-e*
5. *ᵈnin-? ᵈšu-zi-an-na ᵈnin-ma-da ᵈnin-bara ᵈnin-bara*
6. *ᵈnin-zadim ᵈsar-sar-GABA ᵈnin-nigin-na*
7. *tu-tu-a-zu ḫa-ra-ab-gub-bu-ne*
8. *ama-mu za-e nam-bi ù-mu-e-tar ᵈnin-maḫ-e ?-bi ḫé-kéš*
9. *. . . dù-dù nam-lú . . . -ke₄ nam-lú-lu₆-àm . . .*

72. The Louvre tablet is published in *TRS* 71; for the University
Museum tablet, *cf.* notes 68–70.

73. In detail the reconstruction of the lines of the text is as follows:
1–35 = A (= *SEM* 116 + *PBS* X 4, 14 + CBS 2168) i; 6–21 = B
(= *TRS* 71) i; 35–63 = B ii; 58–136 = A ii, iii, iv; 84–104 = B iii;
115–132 = B iv. *Cf. SL* 322 no. 6 and *JAOS* 54.418, which are to be
modified accordingly.

74. For a more detailed comparison of the Semitic poem and its
Sumerian forerunners, *cf.* my comment in *JAOS* 63.69–73.

75. *Cf. ATU* I 4.

76. The text of this epic, known to Babylonians by the name *lugal* (or
lugal-e)-u₄-me-lám-bi-nir-gál, is reconstructed from the following tablets
and fragments: AO 4135 (= *RA* 11.82); *BE XXIX* 2, 3, 6, 7, 8, 10, 13;
BE XXXI 8, 32; CBS 1205, 2161, 2166, 2347, 7842, 7994, 8243, 13876,
15086, 29.13.583, 29.13.699, 29.16.223, 29.16.422, 29.16.439, 29.16.453;
K 133 (= *ASKT* pp. 79 ff.; for duplicate, *cf. ATU I 4*, p. 264); K 1299
(= *ATU I 4*, p. 361); K 2862 + (= *4R* pl. 13 + additions); K 2863
(= *4R* pl. 23, no. 2); K 2871 (= *MVAG* VIII pl. 13; *cf.* pp. 676 ff.);
KAR 13, 14, 17, 25, 363; Ni 1183, 2339, 2743, 2764; *SBH* 71; *SEM* 25,
32, 36, 38; *SRT* 18, 20, 21; VAT 251 (*KGV* pl. 60). In addition to these
49 pieces, 30 published and 19 unpublished, which can now be placed in
their proper position in the epic, we have the following pieces which
probably belong to the poem but are still unplaceable: CBS 8476, 10321,
13103, 15088, 15120; *BE XXIX* 12; K 4827 (= *MVAG VIII* pl. 1); *cf.*
also my comment to *BE XXXI* 9 in *JAOS* 60.239. The following
groups form "joins": 29.16.242 + 29.16.439; 1205 + *BE XXIX* 8; 7842
+ *SEM* 38. Particularly significant and gratifying is the placing of
BE XXIX 2, and 3, which describe the misfortune that befell "the land"
after Ninurta had succeeded in destroying Kur; they begin with approximately line 261 of the epic. For the confusion involved the listing of
the *ᵍⁱˢal* texts as part of this epic (*SEM* p. 3), *cf.* my comment in *JAOS*
60.239, note 15.

77. *Cf. SL* 321, no. 9, and *BASOR* 88.7.   For the corrected reading Ebih, *cf. RA* 31–84 ff.

78. These are *PBS X 4*, 9; *PBS XII* 47; *SEM* 90, 103, 106, 107, 109; *STVC* 42.

79. These are CBS 4256, 29.16.32; Ni 2711, 3052, 4042.

80. *SL* 294–314.

81. *PBS V* 22–24.

82. *BE XXXI* 33–34.

83. *RA* 34.93–134.

84. *SEM* 50, 49, 48.

85. *Cf. RA* 36.78 for nos. 10 and 11; no. 12 will appear in *SLTN*.

86. For no. 13 *cf. BASOR* 79.22–23; for no. 14 *cf. SL* pl. 10.

87. Following is the transliteration and translation of the marked passage on no. 8 of plate XX, which contains the very beginning of the poem:

1. *an-gal-ta ki-gal-šè geštug-ga-ni na-an-gub*
2. *AN an-gal-ta ki-gal-šè geštug-ga-ni na-an-gub*
3. *ᵈinanna an-gal-ta ki-gal-šè geštug-ga-ni na-an-gub*
4. *nin-mu an mu-un-šub ki mu-un-šub kur-ra ba-e-a-e₁₁*
5. *ᵈinanna an mu-un-šub ki mu-un-šub kur-ra ba-e-a-e₁₁*
6. *nam-en mu-un-šub nam-nin mu-un-šub kur-ra ba-e-a-e₁₁*

From the "great above" she set her mind toward the "great below,"

The *goddess*, from the "great above" she set her mind toward the "great below,"

Inanna, from the "great above" she set her mind toward the "great below."

My lady abandoned heaven, abandoned earth, to the nether world she descended,

Inanna abandoned heaven, abandoned earth, to the nether world she descended,

Abandoned lordship, abandoned ladyship, to the nether world she descended.

Following is a transliteration and translation of the marked passage on no. 13 which describes the death of the goddess:

1. *kug-ᵈereš-ki-gal-la-ke₄ ᵍⁱˢgu-za-na i-ni-in-tuš*
2. *ᵈa-nun-na di-kud-imin-bi igi-ni-šè di mu-un-ši-in-kud*
3. *i-bi mu-ši-in-bar i-bi-úš-a-kam*
4. *inim-ma-ne-ne inim-LIPIŠ-gig-ga-àm*
5. *[munus]-tu-ra uzu-níg-sìg-šè ba-an-tu*
6. *uzu-níg-sìg-ga ᵍⁱˢkak-ta lú ba-da-an-lá*
7. *u₄-3 gi₆-3 um-ta-zal-la-ta*

The pure Ereshkigal seated herself upon her throne,

The Anunnaki, the seven judges, pronounced judgment
　　before her,
They fastened their eyes upon her, the eyes of death.
At their word, the word which tortures the spirit,
The sick ["*woman*"] was turned into a *corpse,*
The *corpse* was hung from a *stake.*
After three days and three nights had passed,

　　The poem then continues with the efforts of Inanna's messenger,
Ninshubur, to have the gods bring her back to life.　Enki intervenes and
Inanna is resurrected.　The last three lines of this resurrection passage
read:

1. *60 ú-nam-ti-la 60 a-nam-ti-la ugu-na bi-in-šub-bu-uš*
2. *ᵈinanna ba-gub*
3. *ᵈinanna kur-ta ba-e₁₁-dè*

　　Sixty times, the food of life, *sixty times*, the water of life,
　　　they sprinkled upon it (Inanna's dead body),
　　Inanna arose.
　　Inanna ascends from the nether world.

　　88.　*PBS V 1*; for Poebel's transliteration, translation, and commentary, *cf. PBS IV 1*, pp. 9–70.
　　89.　*SEM 58*; for Chiera's transliteration and translation, *cf. SRT*
pp. 14–23.
　　90.　The text is reconstructed from *SEM 92–93* and *SRT 3*.

a. The date 2000 B. C. assigned to the clay tablets on which the Sumerian compositions are inscribed should be reduced by about 250 years as a result of recent studies which point to a date as low as about 1750 B. C. for Hammurabi, a key figure in Mesopotamian chronology.

b. The number of Sumerian literary tablets and fragments are now known to be approximately five thousand, rather than three thousand. Close to four thousand come from Nippur, if we include the tablets found in the recent joint University Museum-Oriental Institute Expedition (1948–1952). The Sumerian literary tablets in the Hilprecht Collection of the Friedrich-Schiller University (Jena) have been studied by me in the fall of 1955 and again in 1957; for full details see the study "Sumerische literarische Texte in der Hilprecht-Sammlung" (*Wissenschaftliche Zeitschrift der Friedrich-Schiller Universität Jena*, 1955/6, pages 753–763), and *History Begins at Sumer* (see following note) pages 226–236. A first volume of the Hilprecht Collection, consisting of fifty-seven of the more important tablets and fragments will be published in the near future by the Friedrich-Schiller University and the German Academy of Science. The tablets from Ur, as I learned during a stay in London, are over four hundred in number. Most of these have been copied over the years by C. J. Gadd, and will be published in the course of the next few years.

c. The publication of the Sumerian literary works has taken a different form than that projected at the time of the publication of *Sumerian Mythology* (1944). I have since realized that the definitive edition of each of the Sumerian myths, epic tales, hymns, lamentations, essays, and proverb collections, consisting of copies or photographs of the tablets together with transliterations, translations, and commentaries, could not possibly be produced by one man, no matter how concentrated his scholarly efforts, especially since the text of many of the compositions must be pieced together from dozens of individual tablets and fragments scattered throughout the museums the world over. As of today, I have published detailed studies of (1) "Enki and Ninhursag: a Sumerian 'Paradise' Myth"; (2) "Inanna's Descent to the Nether World"; (3) "Inanna and Bilulu" (co-author Thorkild Jacobsen); (4) "Dumuzi and Enkimdu: The Wooing of Inanna"; (5) "Enmerkar and the Lord of Aratta"; (6) "Gilgamesh and the Land of the Living"; (7) "Lamentation Over the Destruction of Ur"; (8) "Schooldays," as well as a number of smaller pieces; for full bibliographical details, see my "Sumerian Literature: A General Survey" in the *Albright Festschrift* now in press. Two important editions of Sumerian compositions to appear in the near future are "Enki and the World Order: The Organization of the Earth and Its Cultural Processes," and "Two Elegies in a Pushkin Museum Tablet," prepared as a result of a recent visit to the Soviet Union. I have also sketched the contents and cited translations from a number of the Sumerian literary compositions in my *From the Tablets of Sumer* (1956), of which a revised and enlarged edition has appeared under the title *History Begins at Sumer* (1959).

In recent years, moreover I have drawn in several younger scholars to prepare definitive editions of a number of Sumerian literary works with my guidance and help. Thus Father Bergmann of the Pontifical Biblical Institute at Rome has prepared for publication "The Deeds and Exploits of Ninurta" (see pp. 79–83 of *Sumerian Mythology*); "The Return of Ninurta to Nippur"; and the large and important "Collection of Temple Hymns." G. Castellino, of the University of Rome, has prepared for publication two hymns of King Shulgi, and a "Hymn to (the sun-god) Utu." Dr. Edmund Gordon, former Research Associate in the University Museum, and now teaching at Harvard University, has prepared for publication a large part of the Sumerian proverbs. As a result of all this scholarly activity, I am planning the publication of a volume entitled *"Sumerian Literature: A Representative Crossection,"* consisting of translations only, of the more important Sumerian literary works, which should prove of fundamental value to the humanist and student of literature and culture in general.

d. A number of important Sumerian inscriptional finds were made during the war-years and afterwards at Harma, Uqair, and Nippur; see my *Iraqi Excavations During the War Years* (*University Museum Bulletin*, vol. XIII, no. 2, pp. 1–29), and "Mercy, Wisdom, and Justice: Some New Documents from Nippur" (*University Museum Bulletin*, vol. XVI, no. 2, pp. 28–39).

e. For a fairly representative cross-section of the Sumerian hymnal material, see now Adam Falkenstein's contribution to *Sumerische und Akkadische Hymnen und Gebete* (1953); see also my review in *Bibliotheca Orientalis* (Leiden) vol. XI, pages 170–176.

f. For a detailed and illuminating sketch of Sumerian "wisdom" literature, see E. I. Gordon's study "A New Look at the Wisdom of Sumer and Akkad" to appear in the coming issue of *Bibliotheca Orientalis* (Leiden).

g. In addition to the "catalogue" tablet discussed there are now six more "catalogues" available; see "Götter-Hymnen und Kult Gesänge der Sumerer auf zwei Keilschrift-'Katalogen' in der Hilprecht Sammlung" (*Wissenschaftliche Zeitschrift der Friedrich-Schiller Universität Jena,* 1956/7, pages 389–395) and the *Introduction to Nos. 53–55* of the forthcoming volume of Sumerian literary texts from the "Hilprecht Sammlung" (see note b above).

h. The dates for the Third Dynasty of Ur and the classical Sumerian period shrould be lowered by about a century; see also note a above.

i For the probable influence of Sumerian literature on the Bible, see my "Sumerian Literature and the Bible" in *Studia Biblica et Orientalia,* vol. III (1959), pages 185–204.

j. For a modification of one of the episodes in this poem based upon tablets which were unknown at the time *Sumerian Mythology* was written, see my "Gilgamesh: Some New Sumerian Data" in the *Proceedings* of the Septième Rencontre Assyriologique Internationale, now in press.

k. The "question and answer passage" can now be restored almost entirely; for details see note 16 of my "Death and the Nether World According to the Sumerian Literary Texts" in a forthcoming volume of *Iraq,* dedicated to Leonard Woolley.

l. The first seven lines of the poem which were omitted altogether in *Sumerian Mythology* because of their fragmentary condition will now be found transliterated and translated in the article mentioned in note j.

m. From the Pushkin Museum tablet inscribed with two elegies (see note c above), we learn for the first time that the Sumerian thinkers held to the view that the sun after setting, continues its journey through the Nether World at night, turning night into day, as it were; and that the moon, too, spends its "day of rest," that is the twenty-eighth day of each month, in the Nether World.

n. A modified interpretation of the first part of the myth will now be found in *History Begins at Sumer,* pages 84–86.

o. Thorkild Jacobsen offers a translation in volume 5 of the *Journal of Near Eastern Studies* which differs significantly from mine, and draws the conclusion that man, after "developing" below the surface of the earth, "shot ˗forth" from the earth through a hole made by Enlil in the top crust of the earth. But his translation of the relevant lines is by no means certain, as I hope to show in a future study of the composition.

p. A full edition of the myth will now be found in *Supplementary Study* No. 1 of the *Bulletin of the American Schools of Oriental Research;* see also *Ancient Near Eastern Texts Relating to the Old Testament* (James Pritchard, Editor) pages 37–40.

q. A definitive edition of this myth will appear in a forthcoming number of the *Wissenschaftliche Zeitschrift der Friedrich-Schiller Universität Jena* (see note c above).

r. For a translation of this "hymnal" myth, see now, Adam Falkenstein in *Sumerische und Akkadische Hymnen und Gebete,* pp. 133–137.

s. Pages 68–75. For another version of the creation of man, suggested by Thorkild Jacobsen, see note o above.

t. For a modified version of this myth see now *History Begins at Sumer,* pages 172–174.

u. For a revised edition of "Inanna's Descent to the Nether World" see now *Journal of Cuneiform Studies,* vol, V, pp. 1–17; for a number of newly identified pieces see my "Death and the Nether World According to the Sumerian Literary Texts" in the forthcoming Woolley Festschrft (see note k).

v. The "Flood" tablet published by Poebel still remains unduplicated.

w. The "Marriage of Martu" tablet published by Chiera still remains unduplicated.

x. For a detailed study of this poem see Journal of Cuneiform Studies, vol. II, pp. 39–70; see also *Ancient Near Eastern Texts Relating to the Old Testament,* pp. 41–42.

INDEX

69 70 71 72 73   12 11 10 9 8 7 6 5 4